THE

LADIES'

HAND-BOOK OF ETIQUETTE

AND

Manual of Politeness.

NEW YORK:
PUBLISHED BY JAMES MILLER,
(SUCCESSOR TO C. S. FRANCIS & CO.)
779 BROADWAY.

PREFACE.

The obvious utility of a work on the plan of that which is now submitted to the public, is such as to require but very few words in the way of preface or apology. In that part of it which relates to Etiquette, the author has endeavoured to give a summary view of the laws relating to the intercourse of society which are clearly established and well understood among persons of polite education. No work of the kind would pretend to *give laws;* but a simple statement of those which prevail among well-bred people, has been attempted; with what success, the intelligent reader will have no difficulty in deciding.

In the advice which forms the concluding portion of the volume, the author has kept utility in view; and has touched upon many topics which, though hitherto neglected in works of this description, are worthy of careful attention from those of the fair sex who deem it important to become graceful in deportment and attractive in manner, as well as intelligent and accomplished.

CONTENTS.

INTRODUCTIONS.

In the introduction of one gentleman to another, great prudence and caution must be used by the really polite man; but in the introduction of ladies to each other, and to gentlemen, infinitely more care is necessary, as a lady cannot shake off an improper acquaintance with the same facility as a gentleman can do, and their character is much easier affected by apparent contact with the worthless and the dissipated.

It is incumbent, therefore, on ladies to avoid all proffers of introductions, unless from those on whom, from relationship or other causes, they can place the most implicit confidence.

INTRODUCTIONS.

As a general rule, ladies may always at once accord to any offers of introduction that may proceed from a father, mother, husband, sister, or brother; those from intimate cousins and tried friends are also to be considered favourably, although not to be entitled to the same implicit reliance as the former.

No person of correct feeling will make an introduction to a lady, without having first apprized her of it, and obtained her consent.

Formerly it was the habit for the ladies to curtsey on being introduced, but this has latterly been changed into the more easy and graceful custom of bowing.

The habit of saluting and shaking hands is now quite obsolete, except in some country towns where ladies at first introductions salute other ladies by kissing them on the cheek, and fervently shake the hands of the gentlemen.

At present, in the best society, all that a lady is called upon to do, upon a first introduction either to a lady or a gentleman, is to make a slight, but gracious inclination of the head.

Upon one lady meeting another for the second or subsequent times, the hand may be extended in supplement to the inclination of the head; but no lady should ever extend her hand to a gentleman, unless she is very intimate,—a bow at meeting and one at parting, is all that is necessary.

Ladies should never bow hastily, but with slow and measured dignity.

If you wish to avoid the company of any one that has been properly introduced, satisfy your own mind that your reasons are correct; and then let no inducement cause you to shrink from treating him with respect, at the same time shunning his company. No gentleman will thus be able either to blame or mistake you.

If, in travelling, any one introduces himself to you, and does it in a proper and respectful manner, conduct yourself towards him with politeness, ease, and dignity; if he is a gentleman, he will appreciate your behaviour—and if not a gentleman will be deterred from annoying you; but acquaintance-ships thus formed must cease where they began, and your entering into conversation with a lady or gentleman in a boat or a coach does not give any of you a right to after recognition. If any one introduces himself to you in a manner betraying the least want of respect, either towards you or himself, you can only turn from him in dignified silence,—and if he presumes to address you further, then there is no punishment too severe.

Be very cautious of giving a gentleman a letter of introduction to a lady; for remember, in proportion as you are esteemed by the lady to whom it is addressed, so do you claim for your friend her good wishes,—and such letters are often the means of settling the weal or the woe of the parties for life. Ladies should never themselves, unless upon cases of the most urgent business, deliver introductory letters, but should send them in an envelope inclosing their card.

to a lady or a gentleman, is to make a slight, but gracious inclination of the head.

Upon one lady meeting another for the second or subsequent times, the hand may be extended in supplement to the inclination of the head; but no lady should ever extend her hand to a gentleman, unless she is very intimate,—a bow at meeting and one at parting, is all that is necessary.

Ladies should never bow hastily, but with slow and measured dignity.

If you wish to avoid the company of any one that has been properly introduced, satisfy your own mind that your reasons are correct; and then let no inducement cause you to shrink from treating him with respect, at the same time shunning his company. No gentleman will thus be able either to blame or mistake you.

If, in travelling, any one introduces himself to you, and does it in a proper and respectful manner, conduct yourself towards him with politeness, ease, and dignity; if he is a gentleman, he will appre-

INTRODUCTIONS.

If any one requests a letter of introduction, and you do not consider that it would be prudent, either in respect to your situation with the person so requesting it, or with the one to whom it would be addressed, refuse it with firmness, and allow no inducement whatever to alter your purpose.

On your introduction to society, be modest, retiring, unassuming, and dignified; pay respect to all, but most to those who pay you the most, provided it is respectful and timely.

Remember that the principal beauty in the female character, is modesty to all, and polite reserve to those you know little regarding; modesty is of itself so beautiful, that it often conquers when a pretty face or a handsome form is overlooked.

Never be afraid to blush when the feeling is genuine, but never affect to blush when you do not feel it—remember that blushing is more frequently the attendant of innocence than of guilt.

Modesty does not only show itself in the face, but also in the dress, and more particularly in the manner, and is always a proof of good and liberal education; no lady can be polite who is not modest and retiring; female politeness is itself the very essence of modesty.

It is much better for a lady to say too little in company than too much; her conversation should always be consistent with her sex and age; and although it may sometimes be bright and witty, yet it should not always be so.

Men frequently look with a jealous eye on a learned woman, and are apt to denominate her a *blue;* be cautious, therefore, in a mixed company of showing yourself too much beyond those around you. To a mind well formed there is more real pleasure derived from the silent consciousness of superiority, than in the ostentatious display of it. It is possible to be silent, and yet not dull,—the silent eyes are often a more powerful conqueror than the noisy tongue; but be not, therefore, apparently careless to the conversation of others,—as the eyes can tell whether you are absent or not, although the mouth gives no audible token of presence.

Avoid all indelicate expressions, and appear not to understand any that may be uttered in your presence. Some ladies not only relish *double entendres*, but actually use them. Yet, however much it may create a feeling of cleverness at the moment, cool reflection is afterwards sure to condemn it both on the part of the speaker and listener. Such discourse, wanton glances, and lightness of carriage, are considered by men as gauntlets to dare them to speak and act in a more free and unguarded manner than they otherwise would have the boldness to do.

Let it be impressed upon your mind, that many ladies have lost their character through a little indiscretion on these heads—and it is as bad with the world to *appear* to have lost caste, as *really* to have lost it.

PROPRIETY OF DEPORTMENT

Propriety of deportment, or *bienseance*, is a happy union of the moral and the graceful, and should be considered in two points of view; it ought, therefore, to direct us in our important duties, as well as in our more trifling enjoyments. When we regard it only under this last aspect, some contend that mere intercourse with the world gives a habit and taste for those modest and obliging observances which constitute true politeness; but this is an error. Propriety of deportment is the valuable result of a knowledge of one's self, and of respect for the rights of others; it is a feeling of the sacrifices which are imposed on self-esteem by our own social relations; it is, in short, a sacred requirement of harmony and affection. But the usage of the world is merely the gloss, or rather the imitation of propriety; and when not based upon sincerity, modesty, and courtesy, it consists in being inconstant in every thing, and in amusing itself by playing off its feelings and ridicule against the defects and excellencies of others. Thanks to custom, — it is sufficient, in order to be recognised as amiable, that she who is the subject of a malicious pleasantry may laugh as well as the author of it.

The usage of the world is, therefore, often nothing more than a skilful calculation of vanity, a futile game, a superficial observance of form, a false politeness, which would lead to frivolity or perfidy, did not true politeness animate it with delicacy, reserve, and benevolence. Would that custom had never been separated from this virtuous amiability! We should then never see well intentioned, and good people, suspicious of politeness; and when victims to the deceitful justly exclaim with bitterness, "This is your woman of politeness!" nor should we ever have made a distinction between the fixed principles of virtue, and what is fit and expedient. The love of good, in a word, virtue, is then the soul of politeness; and the feeling of a just harmony, between our interest and our social relations, is indispensable to this agreeable quality. Excessive gaiety, extravagant joy, great depression, anger, love, jealousy, avarice, and generally all the passions, are too often dangerous shoals to propriety of deportment.

Moderation in everything is so essential, that it is even a violation of propriety itself, to affect too much the observance of it. It is to propriety, its justice and attractions, that we owe all the charm of sociality. At once the effect and cause of civilization, it avails itself of the grand spring of the human mind, self-love, in order to purify and ennoble it; to substitute for pride, and all those egotistical or offensive feelings which it generates, benevolence, with all the amiable and generous sentiments which it inspires. In an assemblage of truly polite people, all evil seems to be unknown; what is just, estimable, and good, or what we call fit or suitable, is felt on all sides; actions, manners, and language, alike indicate it.

And if we place in this select assembly, one who is a stranger to the advantages of a polite education, she will at once be made sensible of the value of it, and will immediately desire to display the same urbanity by which she has been pleased.

If politeness is necessary in general, it is not less so in particular cases. Neither rank, talents, fortune, nor beauty, can dispense with this amenity of manners; nor can anything inspire regard or love, without graceful affability, mild dignity, and elegant simplicity. If all the world feels the truth of the verse which is now a proverb,

"Cette grâce plus belle encore que la beauté,"

every one also is sensible, that grace in conferring

a favour, affects more than the favour itself, and that a kind smile, or an affectionate tone, penetrates the heart more deeply than the most brilliant elocution.

As to the technical part of politeness, or forms alone, the intercourse of society, and good advice, are undoubtedly useful; but the grand secret of never failing in propriety of deportment, is to have an intention of always doing what is right. With such a disposition of mind, exactness in observing what is proper appears to all to possess a charm and influence; and then not only do mistakes become excusable, but they become even interesting from their thoughtlessness and *naïveté*. Be, therefore, modest and benevolent, and do not distress yourself on account of the mistakes of your inexperience; a little attention, and the advice of a friend will soon correct these trifling errors.

AT HOME, AND FROM HOME.

To receive visitors with ease and elegance, and in such a manner that every thing in you, and about you, shall partake of propriety and grace,—to endeavour that people may always be satisfied when they leave you, and be desirous to come again,—are the obligations of the master, and especially of the mistress, of a house.

Every thing in the house ought, as far as possible, to offer solid comfort, and true grace.

Perfect order, exquisite neatness and elegance, which easily dispense with being sumptuous, ought to mark the entrance of the house, the furniture, and the dress of the lady.

In a house where affluence abounds, it is indis

pensable to have a drawing-room; if that canno be afforded, then let the receiving room be the parlour To receive company in a dining-room is not allowed, except among those who cannot bear the expense of furnishing a parlour or drawing-room. Simplicity admitted into an apartment of this kind, suited to smallness of means, we cannot but approve, while we regret, nevertheless the disagreeable things to which such a residence subjects the parties. But we have, in this respect an express warning to hold out to people who give themselves up to it unnecessarily, for it is altogether opposed to the received usages of good society to put yourselves in a situation which you cannot adorn; then you are exposed to receiving twenty visits during dinner, of seeing as many interruptions during the setting of your table, since it is impossible to spread the cloth properly, etc. while strangers remain; finally, of having them witness your domestic cares while removing the remains of a repast, the table-cloth, dishes, etc

Unless from absolute inability, you ought to light your staircase. If the practices of good domestic economy, regulated by the cares of civilization, were more generally extended, an unlighted staircase would not often be found.

After having thus cast a rapid glance into the interior of the house, let us see in what manner it is necessary to receive visitors. When any one enters, whether announced or not, rise immediately, advance towards them, request them to sit down; avoiding, however, the old form of "Take the trouble to be seated," "Come off the door and into the fire," etc. If it is a young man, offer him an arm-chair, or a stuffed one; if an elderly man, insist upon his accepting the arm-chair; if a lady, beg her to be seated upon the sofa. If the master of the house receives the visitors, he will take a chair and place himself at a little distance from them; if, on the contrary, it is the mistress of the house, and if she is intimate with the lady who visits her, she will place herself near her. If several ladies come at once, we give the most honourable place to the one who from age, or other considerations, is most entitled to respect. In winter, the most honourable places are those at the corners of the fire-place: in proportion as they place you in front of the fire, your seat is considered inferior in rank. Moreover, when it happens to be a married lady, and one to whom we wish to do honour, take her by the hand, and conduct her to the corner of the fire-place. If this place is occupied by a young lady, she ought to rise, and offer her seat to the other, taking for herself a chair in the middle of the circle.

A mistress of a house ought to watch anxiously that her guests experience no restraint before her. If a door or window happens to be open in the room in summer time, she should ask of visitors if it incommodes them.

If a lady who receives a half ceremonious visit, is sewing, she ought to leave off immediately, and not resume it, except at the request of the visitor if they are on quite intimate terms, she ought herself to request permission to continue. If a person visits in an entirely ceremonious way, it would be very impolite to work even an instant. Moreover, with friends a lady should hardly be ocupied with her work, but seem to forget it on their account.

In proportion as the visitor is a stranger, the master or mistress of the house rises, and any persons who may be already there, are obliged to do the same. If some of them then withdraw, the master or mistress of the house should conduct them as far as the door. But whoever the person be who departs, if we have other company, we may dispense with conducting them farther than the door of the room. The manner in which we usually re-conduct visitors is regulated in an invariable mode. If it is a lady who is to be accompanied, the master of the house takes her hand, passes it under his arm, and thus leads her as far as the bottom of the stair case, (if the parlour or draw ing room should be on the second floor) unless the steps be so narrow that two cannot go abreast. It is no longer the custom to give the hand to ladies, but to offer them the arm. This new custom does not at all change the ancient rule of propriety which requires, that, in descending a staircase, we should give the side next the wall to the lady whom we accompany; we commonly present to her the right arm, provided, however, that necessity does not oblige us, in order to avoid placing her next the balustrade, to offer the left. If she is to return in a carriage, we should politely hand her into it.

We no longer practise that frank and open hospitality, by virtue of which, in the middle of winter, we request people to refresh themselves with some solid eatables. Such a proposal would now excite a smile; the only refreshment now offered is a glass of wine. When a billet of announcement has informed you, as is customary, that [illegible]eceding invitation on your part will bring guests to your house, you must begin and carefully arrange the apartments you intend for them. They should have a good bed, a bureau, a fire in the winter, and every thing which can contribute to their comfort; a wash-hand basin, water, glass tumblers, &c. every thing which will contribute to neatness, or elegance, ought to be placed in the apartment.

These preliminaries being arranged, a little before the appointed hour of their arrival, you must wait patiently till they come. You should then congratulate them; express the pleasure you enjoy in receiving them, inquire kindly about the incidents of their journey, and request them to make your house their home; this finishes the second series of the duties of hospitality.

The third class of obligations, is assiduity to your guests, otherwise it would seem to them, that their presence is troublesome. To you belongs the care of kindly offering to their view every thing in your house, in the city, or in the country, which is interesting; of making parties in honour of them, as dinner-parties of their friends, or such as it is presumed will please them; these are obligations of hospitality which you cannot omit. When visitors show any intention of leaving you, you ought affectionately to endeavour to detain them; nevertheless, if their resolution seems immoveable, renew your invitations for another visit, and your regret at not having been able to succeed better in retaining them. To do the honours of one's own house, it is necessary to have tact, address, and knowledge of the world, a great evenness of temper, and much affability. It is necessary to forget one's self, in order to be occupied with others, but without hurry or affectation; to encourage timid persons, and put them at their ease; and to enter into conversation, directing it with address rather than sustaining it ourselves. The mistress of a house ought to be obliging, of an equal temper, and attentive in accommodating herself to the particular tastes of every one, especially to appear delighted that guests are with her, and make themselves perfectly at home. They, on their part, should show themselves contented and grateful for the reception that is given; and should immediately on arriving at home, write to the persons who have entertained them, a letter of cordial thanks.

The duties of hospitality are of frequent recurrence, fatiguing, and troublesome, but they are an indispensable obligation. To omit them, is to be willing to pass for a person of no education, and no delicacy; in short, it is to place people in a most embarrassing and painful situation.

At home and abroad the carriage of the body is as expressive as the tone of the voice, and perhaps more so, because it is more constant; it betrays to the observer all the shades of character, and you ought to be very careful of thus making a general confession, by affected manners, a pretending deportment, sneering ways, rough movements a hard countenance, impertinent signs and looks simpering smiles, clownish gestures, a nonchalant and effeminate posture, or a carriage of the body distinguished by prudery and stiffness.

Young ladies, little habituated to the world, ought to be on their guard against excessive timidity, for it not only paralyzes their powers, renders them awkward, and gives them an almost silly air, but it may even cause them to be accused of pride, among people who do not know that embarrassment frequently takes the form of superciliousness.

How often does it happen that timid persons do not notice you at all, or answer in a low voice, and fail in numberless agreeable attentions, for want of courage! These attentions, and these duties, they discharge *in petto*, but who will thank them for it? A proper degree of confidence, but not degenerating into assurance, still less into boldness or familiarity, is then one of the most desirable qualities in the world. To obtain which, you must observe the *ton*, and the manner of polite and obliging people, take them for your guides, and under their direction make continual effort to conquer your timidity.

Good temper, and good nature, are the real essentials to true politeness, and the most artful polish can never impart the "*je ne sais quoi*" of elegance, where these two requisites are wanting.

Propriety in the carriage of the body is especially indispensable to ladies. It is by this that, in a walk, or any assembly, people, who cannot converse with them, judge of their merit and their good education.

How many dancers move off, and how many persons sigh with pity, at the sight of a beautiful woman who has a mincing way, affects grace, inclines her head affectedly, and who seems to admire herself incessantly, and to invite others to admire her also! Who ever makes up his mind to enter into conversation with an immoveable lady, and one who is formal and precise, stretching out the body, pressing the lips, and carrying back the elbows as if they were fastened to her side!

The gait of a lady ought neither to be too quick nor too slow: the most easy and most convenient step is that which fatigues the least, and pleases most. The body and the head should be erect without affectation, and without haughtiness; the movements, especially those of the arms, easy and natural. The countenance should be pleasant and modest.

It is not in good *ton* for a lady to speak too quick or too loud. When seated, she ought neither to cross her legs nor take a vulgar attitude. She should occupy her chair entirely, and appear neither too restless nor too immoveable.

It is altogether out of place for a lady to spread out her dress for display, or to throw her drapery round her in sitting down, as upstarts do to avoid the least rumple. But what is especially to be avoided in ladies is, an unquiet, bold, and imperious air, for it is unnatural, and not allowable in any case. If a lady has cares, let her conceal them from the world, or not go into it. Whatever be her merit, let her not forget, that she may be a man in the superiority of her mind and decision of character, but that externally she ought to appear a woman.

An affectionate, complying, and almost timid aspect, a tender solicitude for those who are about her, should be shown in a lady's whole person. Her face should breathe hope, gentleness, and satisfaction; dejection, anxiety, and ill humour should be constantly banished.

VISITING.

VISITS are a very important part of Etiquette they are not merely the simple means of communication established by necessity, since they have at once for their object, duty and pleasure, but they enter into almost all the acts of life. There are many kinds of visits; the first are the visits on new-years-day; next those of friendship and of ceremony.

At the return of each new-year, custom and duty require us sometimes to present ourselves to our relations first; afterwards to our patrons, our friends, and those who have done any kindness for us. These visits are divided into several classes; those of the afternoon, which are the most polite; of the morning, which are the most friendly and respectful; by cards, and presenting one's self. Visits weekly, which are confined to acquaintances with whom we have not very close relations; monthly, which are no less ceremonious, but, however, partake of coldness; it is at Paris more than at any other place, that these visits are permitted; such calls demand much attention to the toilette; they should be as short as possible; a visit of a quarter of an hour is long enough, and we should be careful to retire when other persons come in.

It would be ridiculous to wish persons a happy new-year, in ceremonious visits.

It is not necessary to mention friendly calls, except to state, that almost all ceremony should be dispensed with. They are made at all hours without much preparation or dressing; a too brilliant attire would be out of place, and if the engagement of the day carry you in such a costume to the house of a friend, you ought obligingly to make an explanation.

Should you not find the person you call on at home, leave a card.

With a friend or relation whom we treat as such, we do not keep an account of our visits. The one who has most leisure, calls upon the one who has the least; but this privilege ought not to be abused; it is necessary to make our visits of friendship at suitable times. On the contrary, a visit of ceremony should never be made without keeping an account of it, and we should even remember the intervals at which they are returned, for it is indispensably necessary to let a similar interval elapse. People in this way give you notice whether they wish to see you often or seldom. There are some persons whom one goes to see once in a fortnight; others, once a month; and others, less frequently.

In order not to omit visits, which are to be made, or to avoid making them from misinformation, when a preceding one has not been returned, persons who have an extensive acquaintance will do well to keep a little memorandum-book for this purpose.

We cannot make ceremonious visits in a becoming manner, if we have any slight indisposition which may for the time affect our appearance or voice, which may embarrass our thoughts, and render our company fatiguing. To take a suitable time for one's self, or for others, is indispensable in visiting, as in every thing else; if you can obtain this by remembering the habits of the person you are going to see, by making arrangements so as not to call at the time of taking meals, in moments of occupation, and when they are likely to be walking. This time necessarily varies; but as a general rule we must take care not to make ceremonious visits, either before the middle of the day or after four o'clock. To do otherwise would, on the one hand, look like importunity, by presenting one's self too early, and on the other might interfere with arrangements that had been made for the evening. After making one's toilette with care, visitors should furnish themselves with cards. Gentlemen ought simply to put their cards into their pocket, but ladies may carry them in a small elegant portfolio, called a card-case. This they can hold in their hand, and it will contribute essentially (with an elegant handkerchief of embroidered cambric,) to give them an air of good taste.

On visiting cards, the address is usually placed under the name, towards the bottom of the card, and in smaller letters. Mourning cards are surmounted with a broad blackmargin; half mourning ones, with a black edge only.

It is bad ton to keep the cards you have received around the frame of a looking-glass; such an exposure shows that you wish to make a display of the names of visitors. When from some cause or other, which multiplies visitors at your house, (such as a funeral or a marriage,) you are obliged to return these numerous calls, it is not amiss to preserve the cards in a convenient place, and save yourself the trouble of writing a list; but if, during the year, your glass is always seen bristling with smoke-dried cards, it will be attributed, without doubt, to an ill-regulated self esteem. If the call is made in a carriage, the servant will ask if the lady you wish to see is at home. If persons call on foot, they go themselves to ask the servants. Servants are considered as soldiers on duty; if they reply that the person has gone out, we should by no means urge the point even if we were certain it was not the case; and if by chance we should see the person, we should appear not to have noticed it, but leave our card, retire, and never call again. When the servant informs us that the lady or gentleman is unwell, engaged in business, or dining, we must by all means retire.

Within fifteen years past, it has been the custom with ladies to take off their hats and shawls; but that supposes an intimacy which would authorize their abstaining from it, at the houses of those with whom they are not much acquainted; and if tney are invited to lay them aside, they should refuse. The short time devoted to a ceremonious visit, the necessity of consulting a glass in replacing the head-dress, and of being assisted in putting on the shawl, prevent ladies from accepting the invitation to lay them aside. If they are slightly familiar with the person they are visiting and wish to be more at ease, they should ask per mission, which should be granted them, at the same time rising, to assist them in taking off their hat and shawl. An arm-chair, or a piece of furniture at a distant part of the room, should receive these articles; they should not be placed upon the couch, without the mistress of the house puts them there.

At the house of a person whom we visit habitual- 'y, we can lay them aside without saying a word, and a lady can even adjust her hair, &c. before the glass, provided she occupies only a few moments r doing it. If the person you call upon is prepar ing to go out, or to sit down at table, you ought, although asked to remain, to retire as soon as possible. The person visited so unseasonably, should, on her part, be careful to conceal her knowledge, that the other wishes the visit ended quickly.

We should always appear delighted to receive visitors; and should they make a short visit, you must express your regret.

Ceremonious visits should be short; if the conversation ceases without being again continued by the person you have come to see, and if she gets up from her seat under any pretext whatever, custom requires you to make your salutation and withdraw. If, before this tacit invitation to retire, other visitors are announced, you should adroitly leave them without saying much. If, while you are present, a letter is brought to the person you are visiting, and she should lay it down without opening it, you must entreat her to read it; she will probably not do so, and this circumstance will warn you to shorten your visit. When you make a half-ceremonious call, and the person you are visiting insists upon your stopping, it is proper to do so, but after a few minutes you should rise to go; if you are urged still further, and are taken by the hands and made to sit down, as it were by force, to leave immediately would be impolite; but, nevertheless, after a short interval, get up a third time, and then certainly retire. To carry children or dogs with one on a visit of ceremony, is altogether vulgar. Even in half ceremonious visits, it is necessary to leave one's dog in the ante-room; the nurse who holds the infant, must also be left without the drawing-room, and this circumstance sufficiently excuses such a suite.

As for animals, it is a thousand times better not to have them at all.

Young married ladies are at liberty to visit by themselves their acquaintances, but they cannot present themselves in public, without their husband or an aged lady. They are at liberty, how ever, to walk with young married ladies or un married ones, while the latter should never walk alone with their companions. Neither should they show themselves, except with a gentleman of their family; and then he should be a near relation of respectable age.

Except in certain provincial towns, where there is a great strictness in behaviour, young married ladies receive the visits of gentlemen; they permit their company in promenades, without suffering the least injury to their reputation, provided it is always with men of good morals, and that they take care to avoid every appearance of coquetry.

Young widows have equal liberty with married ladies.

A lady ought not to present herself alone in a library, or a museum, unless she goes there to study, or work as an artist.

A lady ought to have a modest and measured gait; too great hurry injures the grace which should always characterize her. She should not turn her head on one side and the other, especially in large towns, where this bad habit seems to be an invitation to the impertinent. If such persons address her, she should take good care not to answer them a word. If they persist, she should tell them in a brief and firm, though polite tone, that she desires to be left to herself. If a man follow her in silence, she should pretend not to perceive him, and at the same time hasten a little her step.

After the close of the day, a young lady would conduct herself in an unbecoming manner if she should walk alone; and if she passes the evening with any one, she ought to take care that a domestic comes to accompany her; if not, to request the person whom she is visiting to allow some one to do so. But, however much this may be thought proper, and consequently an obligation, a married lady, well educated, will disregard it, if circumstances prevent her being able, without trouble, to find a conductor.

If the master of the house wishes to accompany you himself, you must excuse yourself politely, from giving him so much trouble; but finish, however, by accepting. On arriving at your house, you should offer him your thanks.

In order to avoid these two inconveniences, it will be well to request your husband, or some one of your relations, to come and wait upon you; you will in this way avoid still another inconvenience. In small towns, where malice is excited by ignorance and want of something to do, they frequently censure the most innocent acts; it is not uncommon to hear slanderous and silly gossips observe, that Madam such a one goes to Madam such a one's, for the sake of returning with her husband. The seeds of such an imputation, once sown, quickly come to maturity.

The care of the reputation of ladies further demands that they should have a modest deportment, should abstain from forward manners, and free speeches

When any one, who is visiting you, has need of a shawl, or handkerchief, offer it with a complaisant zeal, resist the refusal which is made, (and which propriety does not require,) select the best you have, in short, urge the persons not to be in haste to return the articles. If it is very bad weather, and the occasion a proper one, offer your carriage (if you have one!) or an umbrella. The articles thus lent should be returned the next day, by a domestic charged to thank the person for them. But if they are linen, they should not be returned without being washed.

When a lady has borrowed ornaments of another, as, for instance, jewels, the latter should always offer to lend her more than are asked for; she ought also to keep a profound silence about the things which she has lent, and even abstain from wearing them for some time after, in order that they may not be recognised.

This does not allude to more important loans, which are not within the jurisdiction of politeness.

If any accident happens to a borrowed article, we must repair the loss immediately

TABLE.

Politeness ought, as we have seen, to direct and embellish all the circumstances of life; but it is, if possible, still more necessary in relation to pleasures; which without it would have no attraction. It may be said, that dining is almost an event, so many points of propriety has the mistress of the house to observe. When we intend giving an entertainment, we begin by selecting such guests as may enjoy themselves together, or at least tolerate one another. If it is to be a gentlemen's party, there should be no lady present except the lady of the house. The dinner being determined upon, we give out, two or three days beforehand, verbal or written invitations. When we receive a written invitation, we must answer immediately, whether we accept or not, although silence may be considered equivalent to an acceptance. In the latter case, we should give a plausible reason for our declining, and do it with politeness. When the invitation is verbal, we must avoid being urged, for nothing is more weak and disobliging: we ought either to accept or refuse in a frank and friendly manner, offering some reasonable motive for declining, to which we should not again refer. It is not allowable to be urged, except when we are requested to dine with some one whom we have only once seen at the house of a third person, or when we are invited on a visit or other similar occasion. In the former case, if we accept, we should first leave a card, in order to open the acquaintance. Having once accepted, we cannot break our engagement, unless for a most urgent cause. An invitation ought to specify exactly the hour of meeting, and you should arrive precisely at that hour. The table should be ready, and the mistress of the house in the drawing room, to receive the guests. When they are all assembled, a domestic announces that the dinner is served up; at this signal we rise immediately, and wait until the master of the house requests us to pass into the dining-room, whither he conducts us by going before. It is quite common for the lady of the house to act as guide to the guests, while the master offers his hand to the lady of most distinction. The guests also give their arms to the ladies, whom they conduct as far as the table, and to the places which they are to occupy. Having arrived at the table, each guest respectfully bows to the lady whom he conducts, and who in her turn bows also. It is one of the first and most difficult things, properly to arrange the guests, and to place them in such a manner, that the conversation may always be general during the entertainment: we should, as much as possible, avoid putting next one another, two persons of the same profession, as it would necessarily result in an aside dialogue, which would injure the general conversation, and consequently the gaiety of the occasion. The two most distinguished gentlemen ought to be placed next the mistress of the house; and the two most distinguished ladies next the master of the house; the right hand is especially the place of honour. If the number of gentlemen is nearly equal to that of the ladies, we should take care to intermingle them; we should separate husbands from their wives, and remove near relations as far from one another as possible; because, being always together, they ought not to converse among themselves in a general party.

At table, as well as at all other places, the lady, of whatever rank, always takes precedence of the gentleman.

Never refuse taking wine, on being asked,— you are not bound to do more than taste of the wine.

It is not etiquette to wear gloves at table, although some affect *ton* and do so.

The younger guests, or those of less distinction, are placed at the lower end of the table.

As soon as the guests are seated, the lady of the house serves in plates, from a pile at her left hand, the soup, which she sends around, beginning with her neighbours at the right and left, and continuing in the same order.

A mistress of a house ought never to appear to pride herself regarding what is on her table, nor confuse herself with apologies for the bad cheer which she offers you; it is much better for her to observe silence in this respect, and leave it to her guests to pronounce eulogiums on the dinner; neither is it in good ton to urge guests to eat nor to load their plate against their inclination.

If a gentleman is seated by the side of a lady or elderly person, politeness requires him to save them all trouble of pouring out for themselves to drink, of procuring anything to eat, and of obtain ing whatever they are in want of at the table, and he should be eager to offer them what he thinks to be most to their taste.

It would be impolite to monopolize a conversation which ought to be general. If the company is large, we should converse with our neighbours, raising the voice only loud enough to make ourselves heard.

Custom allows ladies at the end of an entertainment to dip their fingers into a glass of water, and to wipe them with their napkins; it allows them also to rinse the mouth, using their plate for this purpose—but custom sanctions in vain what is of itself disgusting.

It is for the mistress of the house to give the signal to leave the table; all the guests then rise, and, offering their arms to the ladies, wait upon them to the door.

We should not leave the table before the end of the entertainment, unless from urgent necessity. If it is a married lady, she requests some one to accompany her; if a young lady, she goes with her mother.

The question whether it is proper, or not, to sing at table, depends now upon the ton of the master of the house. We do not sing at the houses of people of fashion and the high classes of society; but we may do it at the social tables of friends. Here we may repeat what has been said and proved a thousand times, how ridiculous it is to be urged when we know how to sing, or to insist upon hearing a person sing who has an invincible timidity. After dinner we converse, have music, or what is more common, prepare the table for games.

During the week which follows the entertainment, each of the guests owes a visit to the person who has been the entertainer. We usually converse at this time of the dinner, of the pleasure we have enjoyed, and of the persons whom we have met there. This visit has received the cant name of *visite de dig stion.*

SALUTATIONS AND CEREMONIES.

In the first rank of customary formalities, we place those concerning the health.

We shall, necessarily, have little to say on this head; there are, however, some little rules which are not to be neglected. It is proper to vary the phraseology of these formal questions, as much as possible; and we must abstain from them entirely towards a superior, or a person with whom we are but little acquainted, as such inquiries presuppose some degree of intimacy. In the last case, there is a method of manifesting our interest, without violating etiquette; it consists in making these inquiries of the domestics, or of other persons of the house, and of saying afterwards when introduced, '*I am happy, Sir, to hear that you are in good health.'* Custom forbids a lady to make these inquiries of a gentleman, unless he is very ill or very aged. To put a corrective upon this mark of regard, a lady who addresses a gentleman should be earnest in her inquiries of the health of his family, however little intimacy she have with them. Many persons ask this question mechanically, without waiting for the answer, or else hasten to reply, before they have received it. This is in bad ton. Inquiries about the health, it is true, are frequently unimportant, yet they should appear to be dictated by attention and kindness. We must not, however, allow ourselves to be deceived, in mentioning a slight indisposition, to persons who are strangers to us, because their interest can be only formal.

After we are informed of the health of the person we are visiting, it is proper to inquire of them in relation to the health of their families; but it would be wearisome to make a long enumeration of the members. In case of the absence of near re.ations, we ask the person we are visiting, if they have heard from them lately, and if the news is favourable. They, on their part, ask the same of us.

When you are not on visits of great ceremony at the time of taking leave, you are commonly desired to give the compliments and salutations of the persons you are visiting to those with whom you live; then reply briefly, giving them assurances of your regard, &c.

Politeness infuses into visits of some little ceremony, a colouring of modesty, grace, and deference, which should be preserved with the greatest care.

In speaking, it is always proper to give the name of Sir, Madam, or Miss, and if the sentence is somewhat long, the title should be repeated. If the question require a direct answer in the affirmative or negative, we ought never to say roughly, yes or no.

If the person addressed has a title, or that

which he has from his profession, we should give it him, as, *Count*, *Doctor*, &c. In case we meet with many persons of the same profession, we can then distinguish them by adding their name to the title.

A lady will not say, My husband, except among intimates; in every other case she should address him by his name, calling him *Mr.*

It is equally good ton, when alone with him, to designate him by his Christian name.

But when one speaks to a gentleman of the lady to whom he is married, he should not say *your wife*, unless he is intimately acquainted, but *Mrs.* is the most proper. The rules of politeness in this respect, are the same in speaking of the husband.

The custom of ladies curtseying in the street is now perfectly obsolete, except among a few antiquities who use hoops; when a lady sports a hoop, she is then, however, entitled to curtsey—otherwise she is only required to bow.

DRESS.

ATTENTION to one's person, as well as to their reputation, is very necessary. If vanity, pride, or prudery, have frequently given to these attentions the names of coquetry, ambition, or folly, it is no reason why they should be neglected.

The plainest dress is always the most genteel, and a lady that dresses plainly will never be dressed unfashionably.

Next to plainness in every well-dressed lady is neatness of dress and taste in the selection of colours. If a lady does not possess a good eye for colour, she ought never to rely upon her own judgment in the selection of her patterns, or in their arrangement upon her person, else she will be nothing more than a walking violation of all the harmony of light and shade; and however expensively dressed, she will never appear either genteel or fashionable. Propriety requires that we should always be clothed in a cleanly and becoming manner,—even in private, in leaving our bed, or in the presence of no one, it requires that our clothing be in keeping with our fortune, age, and form, as well as with the season, the different hours of the day, and our different occupations.

The most fashionable dress for a lady on first rising from bed, is a small muslin cap, and morning gown of printed cotton. It is well that a half corset should precede the full corset, which last is used only when one is dressed; for it is bad taste for a lady not to be laced at all. The hair papers, if they cannot be removed on rising, should be concealed under a bandeau of lace, or of the hair. They should be removed as soon as may be. In this dress we can receive only intimate friends, or persons who call upon urgent or indispensable business; even then we ought to offer some apology for it. To neglect to take off this morning dress as soon as possible, is to expose one's self to embarrassments often very painful, and to the appearance of a want of education. Moreover, it is well to impose upon yourself a rule to be dressed at some particular hour, (the earliest possible,) since occupations will often present themselves to hinder your getting ready for the day. Disorder of the toilet can only be excused when it occurs rarely, or for a short time,—as in such cases it seems evidently owing to a temporary embarrassment; but if it occur daily, or constantly—if it seems the result of negligence and slovenliness—it is unpardonable, particularly in ladies, whose dress seems less designed for clothing than ornament.

To suppose that great heat of weather will authorize disorder of the toilet, and will permit you to go in slippers, or with your legs and arms bare, or to take nonchalant or improper attitudes, is an error of persons of a low class, or destitute of education. Even the weather of dog-days would not excuse this; and if you would remain thus dressed, you must give directions that "you are not at home." On the other hand, to think that cold or rainy weather will excuse like liberties, is equally an error. You ought not to be in the habit of wearing noisy shoes: this custom is in the worst taste.

However pressed she may be, a lady of good *ton* should not go out in a morning dress, neither with an apron nor cap, even if it is made of fine cloth and trimmed with ribands. We said before, that dress should be adapted to the different hours of the day. Ladies should make morning calls in an elegant and simple ***négligé***, all the details of which we cannot give, on account of their multiplicity, and the numerous modifications of fashion. It is necessary for them when visiting at this time, to arrange their toilet with great care. Still, ceremonious visits, evening visits, and especially balls, require more attention to the dress of the head, and a more brilliant costume. There are head-dresses particularly designed for such occasions, and for no other, such as rich blonde caps, ornamented with flowers, brilliant *barrettes* and toques, appropriate to the drawing-room.

Situation in the world determines among ladies those differences which, though otherwise well marked, are becoming less so every day. Every one knows, whatever be the fortune of an unmarried lady, her dress ought always, in form as well as ornaments, to exhibit less of a *recherché* appearance, and should be less showy than that of married ladies.

Costly cashmeres, very rich furs and diamonds, as well as many other brilliant ornaments, are to be forbidden a young lady; and those who act in defiance of these rational marks of propriety, make us believe that they are possessed of an unrestrained love of luxury, and deprive them selves of the pleasure of receiving these ornaments from the hand of the man of their choice.

All ladies cannot use indiscriminately the privilege which marriage confers upon them in this respect, and the toilet of those whose fortune is moderate should not pass the bounds of an elegant simplicity.

We must beware of a shoal in this case, frequently a young lady of small fortune, desiring to appear decently in any splendid assembly, makes sacrifices in order to embellish her modest attire. But these sacrifices are necessarily inadequate; a new and brilliant article of dress is placed by the side of a mean or old one. The toilet then wants harmony, which is the soul of elegance as well as of beauty. Moreover, whatever be the opulence which you enjoy, luxury encroaches so much upon it, that no riches are ble to satisfy its demands; but fortunately, propriety, always in accordance with reason, encourages by this maxim social and sensible women to appreciate the situation in which they may be placed, and to appear neither too high nor too low. It is alike ridiculous either to pretend to be the most showy, or to display the meanest attire in an assembly.

The rules suitable to age resemble those which mediocrity of fortune imposes;—for instance, old ladies ought to abstain from gaudy colours, *recherché* designs, too late fashions, and graceful ornaments, as feathers, flowers, and jewels. A lady in her decline wearing her hair elaborately dressed, and having short sleeves, and adorned with necklaces, bracelets, &c. offends against propriety as much as against her interest and dignity.

If ladies would wish to appear clothed in good taste and harmony, they ought to adopt in summer light garments and delicate colours, and in winter, furs, thick and warm fabrics, and full colours.

It is superlatively ridiculous for a lady to go

on foot, witn her head dressed or attired for the drawing-room or a ball. If one dwells in a provincial town. where it is not customary to use carriages, they should go in such conveyances as the place affords. Who does not perceive how laughable it is to see a lady, who is clothed in satin, lace, or velvet, laboriously walking in the dust or mud?

Vary your toilet as much as possible, for fear that idlers and malignant wits, who are always a majority in the world, should amuse themselves by making your dress the description of your person.

Certain fashionables seek to gain a kind of reputation by the odd choice of their attire, and by their eagerness to seize upon the first caprices of the fashions. Propriety with difficulty tolerates these fancies of a spoiled child; but it applauds a woman of sense and taste, who is not in a hurry to follow the fashions, and asks how long they will last, before adopting them; finally, who selects and modifies them with success according to her size and figure.

BALLS, CONCERTS, AND EVENING PARTIES.

THESE amusements presuppose a fortune and good *ton;* the practice of society, therefore, and consequently a forgetfulness of the precepts of politeness in respect to them, would be truly preposterous.

When you wish to give a dance, you send out invitations a week beforehand, that the ladies may have time to prepare articles for their toilet

If it is to be a simple evening party, in which we may wear a summer walking-dress, the mistress of the house gives verbal invitations, and does not omit to apprise her friends of this circumstance, or they might appear in unsuitable dresses. If, on the contrary the soirée is to be in reality a ball, the invitations are written, or what is better, printed, and expressed in the third person.

A room appropriated for the purpose, and furnished with cloak-pins to hang up the shawls and other dresses of the ladies, is almost indispensable. Domestics should be there also, to aid them in taking off and putting on their outside garments.

We are not obliged to go exactly at the appointed hour; it is even fashionable to go an hour later. Married ladies are accompanied by their husbands; unmarried ones, by their mother, or by a *chaperon.* These last ladies place themselves behind the dancers; the master of the house then goes before one and another, procures seats for them, and mingles again among the gentlemen who are standing, and who form groups or walk about the room.

A lady cannot refuse the invitation of a gentleman to dance, unless she has already accepted that of another, for she would be guilty of an incivility which might occasion trouble; she would, moreover, seem to show contempt for him whom she refused, and would expose herself to receive in secret an ill compliment from the mistress of the house.

Married or young ladies, cannot leave a ball-room, or any other party, alone. The former should be accompanied by one or two other married ladies, and the latter by their mother, or by a lady to represent her.

Ladies should avoid talking too much; it will occasion remarks. It has also a bad appearance to whisper continually in the ear of your partner.

The master of the house should see that all the ladies dance; he should take notice particularly of those who seem to serve as *drapery* to the walls of the ball-room, (or *wall-flowers*, as the familiar expression is,) and should see that they are invited to dance. But he must do this wholly unperceived, in order not to wound the self-esteem of the unfortunate ladies.

Gentlemen whom the master of the house requests to dance with these ladies, should be ready to accede to his wish, and even appear pleased at dancing with a person thus recommended to their notice.

Ladies who dance much, should be very careful not to boast before those who dance but little or not at all, of the great number of dances for which they are engaged in advance. They should also, without being perceived, recommend to these less fortunate ladies, gentlemen of their acquaintance.

In giving the hand for ladies' chain or any other figures, those dancing should wear a smile, and accompany it with a polite inclination of the head, in the manner of a salutation. At the end of the dance, the gentleman reconducts the lady to her place, bows and thanks her for the honour which she has conferred. She also bows in silence, smiling with a gracious air.

In these assemblies, we should conduct ourselves with reserve and politeness towards all present, although they may be unknown to us.

Persons who have no ear for music, that is to y, a false one, ought to refrain from dancing.

Never hazard taking part in a quadrille, unless you know how to dance tolerably; for if you are a novice, or but little skilled, you would bring disorder into the midst of pleasure. Being once engaged to take part in a dance, if the figures are not familiar, be careful not to advance first. You can in this way govern your steps by those who go before you. Beware, also, of taking your place in a set of dancers more skilful than yourself. When an unpractised dancer makes a mistake, we may apprize him of his error; but it would be very impolite to have the air of giving him a lesson.

Dance with grace and modesty, neither affect to make a parade of your knowledge; refrain from great leaps and ridiculous jumps, which would attract the attention of all towards you.

In a private ball or party, it is proper to show still more reserve, and not manifest more preference for one gentleman than another; you should dance with all who ask properly.

In public balls, a gentleman offers his partner refreshments, but which she very seldom accepts, unless she is well acquainted with him. But in private parties, the persons who receive the company, send round cake and other refreshments, of which every one helps themselves. Near the end of the evening, in a well regulated ball, it is customary to have a supper; but in a soirée, without great preparation, we may dispense with a supper; refreshments are, however, necessary and not to have them would be the greatest impoliteness.

We should retire *incognito*, in order not to disturb the master and mistress of the house; and we should make them, during the week, a visit of thanks, at which we may converse of the pleasure of the ball, and the good selection of the company.

The proprieties in deportment, which concerts require, are little different from those which are recognised in every other assembly, or in public exhibitions, for concerts partake of the one and the other, according as they are public or private. In private concerts, the ladies occupy the front seats, and the gentlemen are generally in groups behind, or at the side of them. We should observe the most profound silence, and refrain from beating time, humming the airs, applauding, or making ridiculous gestures of admiration. It often happens that a dancing soirée succeeds a concert, and billets of invitation, distributed two or three days beforehand, should give notice of it to the persons invited.

Be rarely seen at public places.

Never appear at balls whilst in mourning.

If you give a ball, dance in it rarely.

LETTERS AND PRESENTS.

In writing it is necessary to endeavour to make our style clear, precise, elegant, and appropriate for all subjects. Vivacity of discourse forces us frequently to sacrifice happy though tardy expressions, to the necessity of avoiding hesitation; but what is thus an obstacle in speaking, does not interfere with the use of the pen. We ought therefore, to avoid repetitions, erasures, insertions, omissions, and confusion of ideas, or laboured construction. If we write a familiar letter to an equal or a friend, these blemishes may remain; if otherwise, we must commence our letter again.

The most exact observance of the rules of language is strictly necessary; a fault of orthography or an incorrect expression, is not allowable, even in the least careful letter, or the most unimportant billet. Even correction is not admissible; for, besides being a blemish to the letter, it betrays the ignorance or inattention of the one who writes it.

The choice of materials for writing, without being very essential, is yet necessary; to write on very coarse paper, is allowable only for the most indigent; to use gilt-edged and perfumed paper for letters of business, would be ridiculous.

Many distinguished people, however, reasonably prefer simplicity in this thing, and make use of very beautiful paper, but yet without ornament.

It is extremely impolite to write upon a single leaf of paper, even if it is a billet; it should be always double, although we write only two or three lines. It is still more vulgar to use for an envelope, paper on which there are one or two words foreign to the letter itself, whether they be written or printed.

The rules of politeness ought to decide as to the expense of postage. They require us to defray the expense of the letter, if it is written to distinguished persons, or to those of whom we ask any favour; but it would be an incivility, and sometimes a want of delicacy, to do it when we write to a friend, an acquaintance, or to persons of little fortune, whose feelings we should fear to wound.

It is as indispensable to answer when you are written to, as when you are spoken to, and the indolence which so many correspondents allow in themselves, in this respect, is an incivility. And if, after all, they decide to answer, they begin by apologies so often renewed, that they become commonplace. We must use much care that these excuses may not appear ridiculous. Conciseness and some new terms of expression, are, in this case, indispensable. The same observation is applicable in making use of reproving terms.

Letters supply the place of visits, in bestowing presents, or on occasions of marriages, funerals, etc.; and to neglect to write in such cases, is gross impoliteness.

Two persons should not write in the same letter, by one writing upon the first, and another upon the second leaf, except we are very intimate with the correspondent. The same is applicable to postscripts. The language of men who write to ladies ought always to have a polish of respect, with which the latter ought not to dispense in answering; but on occasions of great ceremony a lady may address to a man such phrases as "I have the honour to be," &c. while he should use the most respectful terms, as "Deign, Madam, to allow me;" "Allow me the honour of presenting you my respects," &c.

You may use a lofty style towards persons to whom you owe respect; an easy, trifling, or even jesting style towards a friend; and a courteous style towards one another generally

If you have many subjects to treat of in the same letter, commence with the most important. for if the person to whom you write is interrupted while reading it, he will be the more impatient to resume its perusal, however little interesting he may find it.

It is useful and convenient to begin a new paragraph at every change of the subject. After having written *Sir* or *Madam* at the top of the letter, we should not commence with one of these phrases,— "*Sir,*" "*Madam,*"—"*Your sister has written me that.*" We should say, "*I understand by a letter which Mrs. ——, your sister, has written me.*"

Take care, also, when writing to a person of great consideration, not to make compliments to any one, but write to this third person whatever you wish him to know.

Titles of respect, as *Lordship, Majesty, Highness, Excellency, Honour, Madam,* &c. ought never to be abbreviated, either in writing to the persons themselves, or to any one who has acquaintance with them.

Figures are used only for sums and dates, numbers of men, days, weeks &c. are to be written at length.

The interior form of a letter has reference to the titles and qualities of persons to whom it is proper to give them; the more or less courteous phrases which we should use; the more or less respectful manner with which the commencement and body of the letter are to be arranged; and the more or less humble terms which we are to use for the signature, the address, or the superscription.

The words *esteem* and *affection* are used only in letters to friends or acquaintance, because they are too familiar; but when accompanied by words which relieve them, they do not offend one. As for example, we can say, "*I am, with profound respect, and the highest esteem,*" &c. The following forms may be used with elegance:

'Accept, Sir, the assurances of high consideration;" "Be pleased to accept the assurances," &c.

The date of a letter may be put at the beginning when we write to an equal; but in writing to a superior, it should be at the end, in order that the title at the head of the letter may be entirely alone. In letters of business, on the contrary, it is necessary to date at the top, and on the first line, that persons may know conveniently the chronological order of their communications.

The date is often necessary to the understand ing of many passages of your letter, to explain the sense of one which your correspondent may have received at the same time from another person: therefore never omit it.

In a simple billet, we put the date of the day, Monday, &c. It is well sometimes to add the hour. Every letter to a superior ought to be folded in an envelope. It shows a want of respect to seal with a wafer,—we must use sealing-wax. Men usually select red; but young ladies use bronze, green, and other colours. Both use black wax when they are in mourning. Except in this last case, the colour of the seal is immaterial, but not the size; for very large ones are in bad taste. The smaller and more *recherché*, the better *ton* they are.

When the letter is closed with or without an envelope, we put only a single seal upon it; but if the letter is large, we use two. Moreover, if it contains important papers, it should have three seals, or more, according to the size of the envelope. If a person takes charge of a letter as a favour, it would be very impolite to put more than one seal upon it. If the letter should be folded in such a manner, that, by partly opening it at the end, its contents may be read, it would be equally impolite to put a little wax upon the edges. We can use this precaution only when the letter is sent by the post or by a domestic.

When we use no envelope, and the third page of the letter is all written upon, we should leave a small blank space on each side, where the seal is to be put; as without this precaution, an important word might be covered.

Persons of taste, who have no coat of arms, adopt a seal bearing some ingenious device.

A letter which is to be shown as a letter of introduction, or recommendation, should never be sealed, when given or sent to the one who is to be the bearer, as he ought necessarily to know the contents. And to seal it without having first allowed the bearer to read it, would be extremely impolite. You should prove to the person recommended, that you have spared no pains to render im a service.

Some distinguished persons are flattered by our omitting, in writing to them, to designate precisely their address. This is an error; we should indicate with exactness, the town, &c., if there is more than one town of the same name. In a large city, it is well to write the name of the street and number, as well as the quarter of the city where the street is. People of business abbreviate this, by putting No, and the number, or the number alone, and this practice is now very general.

It is well to add to the name, the title, or profession, in order to prevent mistake. However, if circumstances have obliged any one of your acquaintance to act in an inferior situation, it would be a want of delicacy, to join his name to that of his business.

In billets, we put the date at the top of the paper, and begin the letter about two inches below. The word *Sir* is put in the first line. We conclude with one of these phrases, *I am, Sir, yours,—I am truly yours, &c.* A billet is not written to ladies, or to superiors, as this was introduced only to avoid ceremony.

The most unceremonious billets, contrary to the common acceptation, are written in the third person. They contain very little, and begin thus, *Mr.* or *Madam, N. present* (*his* or *her*) *respects*, or *compliments, to Mr. Such-a-one,* and requests, &c. After having made the request, we end with, "and will feel obliged."

In this kind of billets, it is best not to use the pronoun *he* or *she;* for, independently of the incivility, it might result in confusion. Sometimes it would be difficult to know, whether the pronoun referred to the person who received the letter, or to the one who wrote it.

In the eyes of persons of delicacy, presents are of no worth, except from the manner in which they are bestowed; strive then to gain them this value.

Presents are offered, first to relations, and to friends, and they occur under different circumstances; on our arrival at a place from which we have been absent for a long time; when our intimate friends leave the town in which we reside, on our return from a journey, particularly to the capital, on marriage days, birth days, days of baptism, or new year's day.

The most delicate presents are the productions of our own industry; a drawing, a piece of needle work, ornamental hair work, &c. But such offerings, although invaluable among friends, are not used on occasions of ceremony.

Presents should excite surprise and pleasure, therefore, you ought to involve them in a little mystery, and present them with an air of joyful kindness.

When you have made your offerings, and thanks have been elicited, do not bring back the conversation to the subject; avoid, particularly, making your gift of consequence. On the contrary, when its merit has been extolled, and the persons who have received the present have evinced a lively satisfaction, say that the gift receives all its value from their opinion of it.

However slight the charm a present may have, or if even insignificant, we should be ill-bred no to manifest much pleasure in receiving it. It is, moreover, necessary, when an opportunity offers, to speak of it, and do not fail of saying to the donor, how useful or agreeable his present is to you. In proportion as a long time has elapsed, this attention is the more amiable, as it proves that you have preserved the object with care. Never give away a present which you have received from another person; or at least so arrange it, that it may never be known.

MARRIAGE.

Let it be impressed upon your mind, that a little more ceremony should be used toward your husband's relations, than towards your own, — with your own relations, you are likely to have been long acquainted, and they are therefore supposed to know all your little peculiarities of character—but in many cases, ladies are suddenly placed by marriage in a new circle, and the utmost respect and caution are necessary, not to offend those who can be made friends or enemies, often by a smile or a frown.

If anything can render politeness ridiculous, and even odious, it is the disposition of certain persons, who in society are moderate, amiable, and gracious; but in private show themselves morose, rough, and ill-natured. This fault, much too common, is one of the greatest inconsistencies of the human mind. Some use all their exertions to please the world, which they only see cursorily, and in which they have only power to procure a few moments of pleasure, and they neglect to be agreeable to their husband, from whom is expected the happiness of a whole life. Perhaps it would be better to be continually capricious, or harsh; for the contrast of politeness in the drawing-room, with the impoliteness at home, makes it appear still more odious. Conjugal intimacy, it is true, dispenses with the etiquette established by politeness, but it does not dispense with attentions.

In the presence of your husband, you ought never to do those things which carry with them a disagreeable idea, nor perform those duties of the toilet, which, before any one but yourself, offend decency and cleanliness.

One ought never to permit disorder in her

husband's wardrobe under the excuse that he is just up, or at his own house.

To dress with neatness and elegant simplicity, is important, even at home.

The conversation at home cannot always be elegant, and sustained in the same manner that it is in society; it would indeed be superlatively ridiculous, that it should not have interruption, or relaxation; but it should be free from all impoliteness and indelicacy.

If at any time the society of your husband causes you *ennui*, you ought neither to say so, nor give any suspicion of the cause, by abruptly changing the conversation.

In all discussions you should watch yourself attentively, lest domestic familiarity raise itself by degrees to the pitch of a quarrel.

To entertain with a politeness particularly affectionate, the friends of the person with whom you are connected by marriage; to respect inviolably the letters which he writes or receives;

to avoid prying into the secrets which he concealς from you; never to act contrary to his inclinations, unless they are injurious to himself, and even in this case not to oppose him, but to endeavour to check them with address and kindness; to beware of confiding to strangers, or to domestics, the little vexations which he causes you; to dread like poison marks of contempt coldness, suspicion, or reproaches; to apologize promptly, and in an affectionate manner, if you have allowed yourself to run into any ill-humour; to receive his counsels with attention, and to execute them as quickly as possible;—these are the obligations of propriety and love, by which married persons of gentleness bind themselves.

There is a still more rigorous duty for new-married persons; they must abstain in public from every mark of affection too conspicuous, and every exclusive attention,

Married persons who, in society, place themselves continually near each other, and who converse and dance together, do not escape the ridi cule to which their feelings blind them.

In society we ought, above every thing, to avoid being personal; for a husband or a wife is another self; and we must forget that self.

SERVANTS.

Much has been said respecting bad servants, and there are a great many bad ones amongst the numerous class; but it is more their misfortune than their fault: they are for the most part taken from a class of society who do not attend properly to the training of their children, and are placed too frequently with those who pay no attention to their comfort.

Treat your servants always with kindness,—but at the same time with firm respect for yourself; on no account be familiar with them, neither hear their tattle, nor tattle with them, and you will have at least a chance of sometimes making them attentive, zealous, and grateful, and of having your services performed with order and alacrity.

Do not scold your servants; you had better turn them away at once. When they need reproof, give them it in a calm, dignified, and firm manner; but on no account, if you can possibly avoid it, find fault with them in the presence of strangers, even though they should let fall the tray with your best set of china upon it.

The *ton* of the mistress of a house is often affected if not measured, by that of her servants; take care, therefore, to make them civil and polite,—teach them to assist your visitors in putting off and on their greatcoats, cloaks, &c.,—and let them always be ready to open the door when your guests arrive or depart.

Accustom your servants never to appear before you too slatternly or too finely dressed; never allow them to enter into conversation with each other in your presence, nor to answer you by signs or coarse terms.

SERVANTS.

If you have only one servant, talk of her by her Christian name; if you have more, talk of them by the names of their offices, such as nurse, cook, housemaid, butler, footman, but always address them by their Christian names.

Although you must avoid all familiar confidential conversation, never speak to your servants with hauteur nor harshness.

Never entertain your visitors with any narrative of your servants' improprieties.

HINTS

ON THE PRESERVATION,

IMPROVEMENT, AND DISPLAY

OF

FEMALE BEAUTY.

THE IMPORTANCE AND UTILITY OF EXERCISE.

THE effect of exercise is, by frequent contraction of the fibres, to brace the muscles and render them stronger, and generally to give more strength to the organs.

Nothing evidently can be more suitable to the organization of woman. Her tissues are soft and flexible; exercise renders them more firm and resisting: her fibres are thin and weak · exercise increases their size and strength: they are moistened with oils aud juices; exercise diminishes the superabundant humidity.

In regard to strength in general, it may be observed that, in the present state of society, we have less need of it than the people of ancient times. Muscular strength is a kind of superiority no longer in such favour, and the aim of gymnastics is consequently nothing more than to endow the body with all the strength, vigour and activity, compatible with health, without injury to the development of the intellectual faculties.

Moreover, the education which is suited to the male, is not calculated to render the female amiable and useful in society.

This is an observation of all times. The ancients were too good observers not to know that women, by her less stature, her weaker organization, her predominant sensibility, and her peculiar function of multiplying the species, was not destined by nature to such toilsome labours as men.

We seek, accordingly, to develop in woman that modesty and gentleness which are proper to her, that soft and attractive air which characterizes her, and those pleasing graces which distinguish her.

The constitution of women, indeed, bears only moderate exercise. Their feeble arms cannot support severe and long-continued labour. It renders them meagre, and deforms the organs, by compressing and destroying that cellular substance which contributes to the beauty of their outlines and of their complexion. The graces accommodate themselves little to labour, perspiration and sun-burning.

We must not, however, conclude from this, that females should be kept in a state of continual repose, or that the delicacy of their organization prevents their taking exercise.

It is a fact that labour, even the most excessive, is not so much to be feared as absolute idleness. The state of want which forces some women of the lowest class to perform labours that seem reserved for men, deprives them only of some attractions. Excessive indolence, on the contrary, destroys at once health and that which women value more than health, though it never can subsist without it, namely, beauty.

The more robust state of health in females brought up in the country, is attributable to the exercise they enjoy. Their movements are active and firm; their appetite is good, and their complexion florid; they are alert and gay; they know neither pain nor lassitude, although they are in action without cessation under all kinds of weather. It is exercise which gives them vigour, health and happiness—exercise to which they are so frequently subjected, even in infancy and youth.

We observe also, that in a family where there are several sisters of similar constitution, the one who from circumstances has been accustomed to regular and daily exercise, almost always possesses most strength and vigour.

Mothers and teachers, therefore, instead of fearing that their children should fatigue themselves by exertion in active sports, should subject them early to it. They will thus give them more than merely life and instruction; they will confer on them health and strength.

But some mothers are afraid to see their daughters entering with spirit into exercises, and are of opinion that health cannot be obtained without sacrificing the graces which a female who is intended for society should possess.

They may rest assured that no recommender of exercise would endeavour to make a stout robust woman of a little, delicate and nervous girl, or would prescribe for her the female gymnastics of the half-naked women of Lacedemon, as instituted by Lycurgus.

What we can, and what we should endeavour to do, is to obtain a good constitution, absence from all deformity, and sufficient strength to prevent the display of vicious sensibility, but not to destroy that delicacy and those attractions which constitute beauty and grace.

But it may be feared that the peculiar structure and the natural weakness of woman, may render dangerous the exercises intended to combat it.

Those who make such objections should recollect that the circumstances which distinguish the sexes, and which modify them, remain imperfect and without action, until the age of puberty, and that children of both sexes have nearly the same appetites, the same wants, and the same inclinations. It is hence we recognise in them nearly the same physiognomy, a similar tone of voice, and similar manners.

This will be the less surprising when it is known that the internal organization, even the structure of the bones, has a greater resemblance in early life than at a subsequent period. Thus until they arrive at maturity, the pelvis or basin is rarely larger than in youths. Hence all the exercises which depend upon position and walking will not be more difficult for them than for boys; while, for full-grown women, these exercises are more difficult and embarrassing.

This community of structure, as well as the fact that, at this early age, activity, restlessness and the desire of motion are remarkable in girls, all point out the danger of repose.

Instead, therefore, of being afraid of exercise for young girls, they should be subjected to it as soon as possible: and, when this is the case, they uniformly prove the truth of the observation, made by teachers of exercises, that females, in agility, precision and address, surpass boys of the same age.

So much for the effects of exercise upon the locomotive system.

With regard to the vital or nutritive system, it is not less certain that exercise augments the circulation and respiration, and perfects the formation of the blood and the nourishment of the body, in the same proportion in which the power of the lungs is developed.

By carrying toward the exterior the forces which, during a state of repose, tend almost always to concentrate themselves either in the brain or in the abdominal organs, exercise makes of these forces a more exact distribution, re-establishes or maintains their equilibrium, and, by exciting the circulation, provokes the insensible perspiration, without which health and beauty are impossible.

In regard to the mental system, exercise, while it increases the activity of the muscles, prevents, as we have seen, the vicious predominance of the sensitive system. Diseased sensibility can never exist where the constitution has not been suffered to become enervated by indolence. When external agitation employs our faculties, the interior reposes.

If already the defective power of the mental functions tends to too vivid mobility, exercise gives them more of the stability of energy. The nervous susceptibility, which is increased by weakness, is reduced to its proper degree, as soon as exercise has strengthened the organs. By this useful diversion, the affections of the heart are calmed. "Otia si tollas, periere Cupidinis arcus."

But this is not all: by diminishing the causes of exaggeration in the affections and passions, mildness and goodness, the most certain sources of happiness, remain in conjunction with health.

There can, therefore, be no doubt of the utility of exercise in remedying whatever may be defective in the female organization, and laying the foundation of a constitution exempt from infirmities and disease.

APPROPRIATION OF EXERCISE.

Exercise is not equally useful in all climates.

In warm climates, heat, by calling the vital forces towards the circumference, supplies the place of exercise in many respects; and the debilitating perspirations which excite too greatly even without exercise, may render that often pernicious.

Exercise should, doubtless, be varied according to the sex of the individual.

It would, however, be a prejudicial error to suppose that females should be subjected only to passive exercise. On the contrary, the sedentary occupations of women impose upon them, more than on men, the necessity of engaging in active exercises.

Exercises should only be more moderate in woman than in man. A female, moreover, will with advantage, use those that act upon the muscles of the chest, which her mode of life affords but few opportunities of exercising.

Exercise should vary according to age.

Temperament requires to be studied in the selection of exercises.

An individual possessed of a sanguine temperament should constantly use active exercises. If sanguification or the formation of blood be very active, they may be carried so far as to produce perspiration. It is the best means of dissipating, to the advantage of the nutrition of the muscles, the excess of plethora, and superabundance of juices, which torment persons of this temperament.

Such persons ought, however, to abstain from exercises that require great efforts, on account of their predisposition to aneurisms, hemorrhages, and cerebral effusions and compressions.

Passive exercises, or those methods that gently strengthen the fibres without causing any corresponding loss, and thus induce plethora, would be unsuitable to sanguine persons disposed to hemorrhage.

Active exercises suit individuals of a lymphatic temperament, naturally dull, slow and indolent.

The ancients remarked the good effects of exercise upon girls of weak constitutions, of soft and lax texture, subject to languid maladies; and they accordingly applied exercise in the cure of many diseases that baffled the skill of the physician. The moderns have profited by their observations, and made new ones of similar tendency.

It would, however, be imprudent to subject suddenly to violent exercise young girls of feeble constitution, with soft skin, pale complexion, and light hair, which are proofs of weakness.

In persons also with soft fibres, whose narrow and feeble vessels are plunged in fat, exercise must be very moderate, in order not radically to wear out muscular forces deprived of primitive energy. If it is very violent, or is continued too long, it may then sometimes occasion adipose inflammations of the viscera.

To remedy this languishing state, their fibres should first be braced by passive exercises frequently repeated, commencing by those which are extremely gentle. Exercise in the open air, such as carriage-riding, is particularly useful to girls of this constitution. The force and resistance of the fibres will augment in proportion as the fatty and serous plethora dissipates itself.

A nervous temperament promises superiority of the mental faculties; but it may become the source of great evils, if we do not diminish that exquisite susceptibility which sooner or later would produce them.

The general effect of exercise is to strengthen the body and counteract the early predisposition to a nervous temperament. This temperament indeed requires continual exercise. In it, there is no danger that, in strengthening the body, we may injure those faculties that seem to arise from a nervous temperament. With such constitution, no one can ever become an athlete, which as we know, is converting mind into brute force. Nervous girls, then, should be strengthened; it will prevent them becoming invalids: it is certain they will remain clever.

A physician accordingly observes that, in strengthening the animal economy by exercise, we get rid of the nervous irritability, the sickly sensibility, which is the offspring of luxury, and parent of vapours, hysterics and hypochondria, as well as of the fatal practices which attack the sources of life, and which commence at the age of puberty and often sooner. By strengthening the muscles, exercise moderates this vicious sensibility. Exercise produces lassitude, and lassitude sleep; and when a person sleeps soundly, she will not be awakened by the fancies of a disordered imagination.

Passive, mixed, and moderately active exercises suit a bilious temperament, characterized by dryness and extreme rigidity of fibre. The individual should use moderate and sustained exercise, fit rather to regulate than accelerate the march of functions already too rapid.

Particular dispositions also require particular exercises. One cannot endure the motion of the most easy carriage; another suffers from that of a boat; a third finds it impossible to ride on horseback, &c. It is sometimes desirable to combat these dislikes, but we must not obstinately endeavour to surmount them, when they appear determined: it is better, in such a case, to discontinue the exercise disliked: and frequently another, even more active, will not produce the same inconvenience.

The habits previously contracted should not be overlooked in advising as to exercise. A young girl whose condition is sedentary, should not be subjected to such exercise as a young man who is generally actively employed. The best application of gymnastics, is that which conducts the pupil gradually from the most gentle exercise to the most active.

Without speaking of acute maladies, in which muscular action is always hurtful, there are different states of the body in which the utility of exercise is very doubtful: there are even some in which, by the nature of its direct effects, it can do only ill. Such is the case with young girls who may be affected with predisposition to apoplexy, asthmatical diseases, &c.

It is evident that in general passive exercises only should be had recourse to in case of sickness and indispositions, because spontaneous movement might then be more or less injurious.

Exercise, however, if properly directed, is extremely beneficial in convalescence. The recovering patient who cannot yet walk across her chamber, should be carried or wheeled in an easy chair, until she can support the motion of a carriage.

Many chronic affections are favourably influenced by exercise; but of course it must be taken under the precautions we have mentioned for convalescents. In these cases and others analagous, where passive exercises are useful, it rarely happens that the use of active exercises is successful.

The same does not hold in scrofulous cases, where debility, paleness, and want of elasticity indicate the necessity of motions as active as the strength will admit. It is probable that these diseases, so common in infancy and youth, will be very rare in children who are regularly trained to exercise.

PARTICULAR DIRECTIONS

FOR THE

PRESERVATION AND IMPROVEMENT OF BEAUTY.

THE preservation of an agreeable complexion (which always presupposes health) is not the most insignificant of exterior charms. Though we yield due admiration to regularity of features (the Grecian contour being usually so called,) yet when we consider them merely in the outline, our pleasure can go no farther than that of a cold critic, who regards the finely-proportioned lineaments of life as he would those of a statue. It is complexion that lends animation to a picture; it is complexion that gives spirit to the human countenance. Even the language of the eyes loses half its eloquence, if they speak from the obscurity of an inexpressive skin. The life-blood in the mantling cheek; the ever-varying hues of nature glowing in the face, "as if her very body thought;" these are alike the ensigns of beauty and the heralds of the mind; and the effect is, an impression of loveliness, an attraction, which fills the beholder with answering animation and the liveliest delight:

"'Tis not a lip or eye we beauty call,
But the joint force and full result of all."

As a Juno-featured maid with a dull skin, by most people will only be coldly pronounced *critically* handsome; so a young woman with very indifferent features, but a fine complexion, will from ten persons out of twelve, receive spontaneous and warm admiration.

The experience (when once we admit the proposition that it is *right* to keep the casket bright which contains so precious a gem as the soul) must induce us to take precautions against the injuries continually threatening the tender surface of the skin. It may be next to an impossibility, to change the colour of an eye, to alter the form of the nose, or the turn of the mouth; but though heaven has given us a complexion which vies with the flowers of the field, we yet have it in our power to render it dingy by neglect, coarse through intemperance, and sallow by dissipation.

Such excesses must therefore be avoided; for though there may be a something in the pallid cheek which excites interest, yet, without a certain appearance of health, there can never be an impression of loveliness. A fine, clear skin, gives an assurance of the inherent residence of three admirable graces to beauty; Wholesomeness, Neatness, and Cheerfulness. Every fair means ought to be sought to maintain these vouchers for not only health of body, but health of mind.

I have already given some hints to this purpose; at least as far as relates to the advantage resulting to young females from exercise. Those which affect the heart, and point through time into eternity, must not be less observed; for unless its thoughts are kept in corresponding order and the passions held in peace, all pre-criptions will be vain to keep those boiling fluids in check, which, in spite of Roman fard and balm of Mecca, will spread themselves over the skin, and there exhibit an outward and visible sign of the malignant spirit within. But, independently of these mental causes of corporeal defect, disorders of the skin, arising from accidental circumstances, are very frequent in the United States, owing to the extraordinary vicissitudes of our climate, — where a difference of forty degrees in the range of the thermometer within the space of twenty-four hours, is quite a common occurrence. The fashions of the day are likewise in a very high degree inimical to health and beauty. The changes of the temper-ture, by abruptly exciting or repressing the regular secretions of the skin, roughen its texture, injure its hue, and often deform it with unseemly, though transitory eruptions. All this is increased by the habit ladies have of exposing themselves unveiled, and frequently without bonnets, in the open air. The head and face have then no defence against the attacks of the surrounding atmosphere, and the effects are obvious. The barouche, for this reason, and the more consequential one of subjecting its inmates to dangerous chills, is a fatal addition to the variety of our equipages. Our autumnal evenings, with this carriage and our gossamer apparel, have already sent many young females to untimely graves.

To remedy these evils, I would strenuously recommend, for health's sake, as well as for beauty, that no lady should make one in any riding, airing, or walking party, without putting on her head something capable of affording both shelter and warmth. Shakspeare, the poet of the finest taste in female charms, makes Viola regret having been obliged to "throw her sun-expelling mask away!" Such a defence I do not pretend to recommend; but I do consider a veil a useful as well as elegant part of dress, it can be worn to suit any situation; open or close just as the heat or cold may render it necessary.

The custom which some ladies have, when warm, of powdering their faces, washing them with cold water, or throwing off their bonnets, that they may cool the faster, are all very injurious habits. Each of them is sufficient (when it meets with any predisposition in the blood) to spread an eruption over the skin, and make a once beautiful face hideous for ever.

The person, when overheated, should always be allowed to cool gradually, and of itself, without any more violent assistant than, perhaps, the gentle undulation of the neighbouring air by a fan. Streams of wind from opened doors and windows, or what is called *a thorough air*, are all bad and highly dangerous applications. These impatient remedies for heat are often resorted to in balls and crowded assemblies; and as frequently as they are used, we hear of sore throats, coughs, and fevers. While it is the fashion to fill a drawing-room like a theatre, similar means ought to be adopted, to prevent the ill effects of the consequent corrupted atmosphere, and the temptation to seek relief by dangerous resources. Instead of the open balcony and yawning door, we should have ventilators in every window,—and thus feel a constant succession of pure and temperate air.

Excessive heat, as well as excessive cold, is apt to cause distempers of the skin; and as the fine lady, by her strange habits, is as prone to such changes as the desert-wandering gipsy, it is requisite that she should be particularly careful to correct the deforming consequences of her fashionable exposures. At her usual ablution, night and morning, nothing is so fine an emollient for any rigidity or disease of the face as a wash of French or white brandy, and rose-water, the spirit making only one-third of the mixture. The brandy keeps up that gentle action of the skin which is necessary to the healthy appearance of its parts. It also cleanses the surface. The rose-water corrects the drying property of the spirit, leaving the skin in a natural, soft, and flexible state. Where white or French brandy cannot be obtained, half the quantity of spirits of wine will tolerably supply its place.

The eloquent effect of complexion will, I hope, my fair friends, obtain your pardon for my having confined your attention so long to what is generally thought (though in contradiction to what is felt) a trifling feature, if so I may be allowed to name it.

I am aware of your expectations, that I would give the precedence, in this dissertation, to the eye. I subscribe to its super-eminent dignity, for none can deny that it is regarded by all nations as the faithful interpreter of the mind, as the window of the soul, the index in which we read each varied emotion of the heart; it is indeed the "spirit's throne of light." But how increased an expression does this intelligent feature convey, when aided by the glowing tints of an eloquent complexion! Indeed, it is the happy coincidence of the eye and the complexion which forms the strongest point of what the French call *contenance.*

The animated changes of sensibility are nowhere more apparent than in the transparent surface of a clear skin. Who has not perceived, and admired, the rising blush of modesty enrich the cheek of a lovely girl, and, in the sweet effusion, most gratefully discern the true witness of the purity within? Who has not been sensible to the sudden glow on the face, which announces, ere the lips open, or the eye sparkles, the approach of some beloved object? Nay, will not even the sound of his name paint the blooming cheek with deeper roses?

> "Who hath not own'd, with rapture-smitten frame,
> The power of grace, the magic of a name?"

Shall we reverse the picture? It has been seen how the soul proclaims her joy through its wondrous medium:—shall she speak her sorrows too? Then let us call to mind, who have beheld the deadly paleness of her who learns the unexpected destruction of her dearest possessions!—Perhaps a husband, a lover, or a brother, mingled with the slain, or fallen, untimely, by some dreadful accident. Sudden partings like these

> "Press the life from out young hearts."

We see the darkened, stagnant shade which denotes the despair-stricken soul. We behold the livid hues of approaching frenzy, or the blacker stain of settled melancholy! Heloisa's face is paler than the marble she kneels upon In all cases the mind shines through the body; and according as the medium is dense or transparent, so the light within seems dull or clear.

Advocate as I am for a fine complexion, you must perceive, that it is for the *real,* and not the *spurious.* The foundation of my argument, *the skin's power of expression,* would be entirely lost, were I to tolerate that fictitious, that dead beauty, which is composed of white paints and enamelling. In the first place, as all applications of this kind are as a mask on the skin, they can never, but at a distant glance, impose for a moment on a discerning eye. But why should I say a *discerning eye?* No eye that is of the commonest apprehension can look on a face bedaubed with white paint, pearl-powder, or enamel, and be deceived for a minute into a belief that so inanimate a "whited wall" is the human skin. No flush of pleasure, no shudder of pain, no thrilling of hope, can be descried beneath the encrusted mould: all that passes within is concealed behind the mummy surface. Perhaps the painted creature may be admired by an artist as a well-executed picture; but no man will seriously consider her as a handsome woman.

White painting is, therefore, an ineffectual, as well as dangerous practice. The proposed end is not obtained; and, as poison lurks under every layer, the constitution wanes in alarming proportion as the supposed charms increase.

The use of red paint upon the cheek, although not generally so deleterious as the white, is yet to be avoided by every respectable lady. The practice is objectionable even when it goes no further than a slight tinge of vegetable rouge upon the cheek of pallid beauty. But what language of censure can sufficiently express the condemnation of its habitual and immoderate use? A violently rouged woman is one of the most disgusting objects to the eye. The excessive red on the face gives a coarseness to every feature, and a general fierceness to the countenance, which transforms the elegant lady of fashion into a vulgar harridan.

The same censure is applicable to the practice of pencilling and painting the eyebrows. Such clumsy tricks of attempted deception can scarce excite other emotion in the mind of the beholder, than contempt for the bad taste and wilful blindness which could ever deem them passable for a moment. There is a lovely harmony in nature's tints, which we seldom attain by our added chromatics. The exquisitely fair complexion is generally accompanied with blue eyes, light hair and light eye-brows and lashes. So far all is right. The delicacy of one feature is preserved in effect and beauty by the corresponding softness of the other. A young creature, so formed, appears to the eye of taste like the azure heaven seen through the fleecy clouds on which the brightness of day delights to dwell. But take this fair image of the celestial regions, draw a black line over her softly-tinctured eyes, stain their beamy fringes with a sombre hue, and what do you produce? Certainly a fair face with *dark* eye-brows! But that feature, which is an embellishment to a brunette, when seen on the forehead of the fair beauty, becomes, if not an absolute deformity, so great a drawback from her perfections, that the harmony is gone; and, as a proof, a painter would immediately turn from the change with disgust.

Nature, in almost every case, is our best guide Hence the native colour of our own hair is, in general, better adapted to our own complexions than a wig of a contrary hue. A thing may be beautiful in itself, which, with certain combinations, may be rendered hideous. For instance, a golden-tressed wig on the head of a brown woman, makes both ridiculous. By the same rule, all fantastic tricks played with the mouth or eyes, or motions of the head, are absurd, and ruinous to beauty. They are solecisms in the works of nature.

In Turkey, it happened to be the taste of one of its great monarchs, to esteem large and dark-lashed eyes as the most lovely. From that time, all the fair slaves of that voluptuous region, when nature has not bestowed "the wild-stag eye in sable ringlets rolling," supply the deficiency with circles of antimony; and so, instead of a real charm, they impart a strange artificial ghastliness to their appearance.

The English women, in like manner, when a celebrated *belle* came under the pencil of Sir Peter Lely, who exhibited to her emulative rivals the sweet peculiarities of her long and languishing eye, they must needs all have the same; and not a lady could appear in public, be her visual orbs large or small, bright or dull, but she must affect the soft sleepiness, the tender and slowly-moving roll of her subduing exemplar. But though Sir Peter's gallant pencil deigned to compliment his numerous sitters by drawing their strained aspect after the model of the peerless *belle*, yet, in place of the nature-stamped look of modest languishment, he could not but often recognise the disgraceful leer and hideous squin Let every woman be content to leave her eye as she found them, and to make that use of them which was their design. They were intended to see with, and artlessly express the feelings of a chaste and benevolent heart. Let them speak this unsophisticated language, and beauty will beam from the orb which affectation would have rendered odious.

Analogy of reasoning will bring forward similar remarks with regard to the movements of the mouth, which many ladies use, not to speak with or to admit food, but to show dimples and display white teeth. Wherever a desire for exhibition is discovered, a disposition to disapprove and ridicule arises in the spectator. The preten tensions of the vain are a sort of assumption ove others, which arms the whole world against them

PECULIARITIES

IN

FEMALE CARRIAGE AND DEMEANOUR,

Best suited to the Display of

BEAUTY AND GRACE.

"By her graceful walk, the Queen of Love is known."
VIRGIL.

As order is the harmonizer of the universe, sc consistency is the graceful combiner of all that is beautiful in woman.

In reference to this sentiment, her manners must bear due affinity with her figure, and her deportment with her rank. The youthful and delicate-shaped girl is allowed a gaiety of air which would ill-become a woman of maturer years and larger proportions; but at all times of life, when the figure is slender, the neck swan

.ike, and the motions naturally swaying, for that girl, or that woman, to affect what is called a majestic air, would be as unavailing as absurd. It is not in the power of a figure so constructed ever to look majestic. By stiffening her joints, walking with an erect mien, and drawing up her neck, she would certainly be upright; she would seem to have had a determined dancing-master, who, in spite of nature and grace, had made her *hold up her head;* but she would never look like any thing but a stiff, inelegant creature. The character of these slight forms corresponds with their resemblances in the vegetable world; the aspen, the willow, bend their gentle heads at every passing breeze, and their flexible and tender arms toss in the wind with grace and beauty; such is the woman of delicate proportions. She must enter a room either with the buoyant step of a young nymph, if youth is her passport to sportiveness; or, if she is advanced nearer the meridian of life, she then may glide in, with that ease of manner which gives play to all the graceful motions of her elegantly undulating form For her to crane up her neck, would be to change its fine swan-like bend into the scraggy throat of the ostrich: all her movements should be of a flexible character. Her mode of salutation should be rather a bow than a curtsey; and when she sits, she should model her easy attitude rather by the ideas of the painter when he would pourtray a reclining nymph, than according to the lessons of the grace-destroying governess, who would marshal her pupils on their chairs like a rank of drilled recruits. In short, for a slender, or thin woman, to be stiff at any time, is, in the first case, to render of no effect the advantages of nature; and, in the next, to increase and aggravate her defects, by making it more conspicuous by a constrained and ridiculous carriage.

Though we cannot unite the majestic air which declares command with this easy, nymph-like deportment, the dignity of modesty may be its inseparable companion. The timid, the retreating step, the downcast eye; the varying complexion, "blushing at the deep regard she draws!" all these belong to this class of females; and they are charms so truly feminine, so exquisitely lovely, that I cannot but place them with their counterpart, the ethereal form, as the perfection of female beauty.

The woman whose figure bears nature's own stamp of majesty, is generally of a stately make; her person is squarer, and has more of *embonpoint* than the foregoing. The very muscles of her neck are so formed as to show their adaptation to an erect posture. There is a sort of loftiness in the natural movement of her head, in the high swell of her expansive bosom. The step of this woman should be grave and firm; her motions few and commanding; and the carriage of her head and person erect and steady. An excess in stateliness could not have any worse effect on her, than perverting the majesty of nature into the haughtiness of art. We might admire or revere the first; the last we would probably resent and detest. The dignified beauty must therefore beware of overstraining the natural bent of her character: it is like the bombast of exalted language, which never fails to lose its aim, and engender disgust. We might laugh at a delicate girl, so far exaggerating the pliancy of her form and ease of manners, as to twist herself into the thousand antics of a Columbine; she aims at pleasing us, and though she chooses the wrong method, we will not frown, but only smile at the ridiculous exhibition. But when a majestic fair one presumes to arrogate an undue consequence in her air, it is not to gratify our senses that she assumes the extraordinary diadem; and, irritated at the contempt her greatness would wish to throw upon us inferior personages, we treat her like an usurper; and, armed with a sense of injustice, we determine to pull her at once from her throne.

The easy, graceful air, we see, belongs exclusively to the slender beauty, and the moderated majestic mien to a greater *embonpoint.*

There is a race of women whose persons have no determined character. These must regulate and adopt their demeanours according to the degrees in which they approach the two before-mentioned classes. But in all cases, let it never be forgotten, that a too faint copy of a model is better than an overcharged one. Excess is always bad. Moderation never offends. By falling easily into the degree of undulating grace or the dignified demeanour which suits your character, you merely put on the robe which nature designed, and the habit will be fit and becoming.

But when the nymph-like form assumes a regal port, or a commanding dame pretends to "skip and play," the affectation on both sides is equally absurd: discords of this kind are eve. ridiculous and odious. Besides these, there are affectations of other descriptions of equal folly and bad effect. Some ladies, to whom nature has given a good sight, and lovely orbs to look through, must needs pretend a kind of half-blindness, and they go peeping about through an eye-glass dangling at the end of a long gold chain, hanging at their necks. Not content with this affectation of one defect, they assume another, and lisp so inarticulately, that hardly three words in a sentence are intelligible. All such follies as these are not more a death-blow to all respect for the novice that plays them off, than they are sure antidotes to any charms she may possess. Simplicity is the perfection of form; simplicity is the perfection of fine dressing; simplicity is the perfection of air and manners.

In the details of carriage we must not omit a due attention to gait, and its accompanying air. We find that it was "by her *graceful walk* the Queen of Love was known!" In this particular, the French women far exceed us. Pope observes, that "they move easiest who have learnt to *dance*." And it is the step of the highly-accomplished dancer that we see in the generality of well-bred Frenchwomen; not the march of the military sergeant, which is the usual study with our pedestrian Graces.

Both in the case of air and gait, it is necessary to begin early to train the person and the limbs to the ease and grace you wish. It is difficult to straighten the stem long left to diverge into irregular wildness; but the tender tree, pliant in youth, needs only the directing hand of a careful gardener to train it to symmetry and luxuriance.

Many of the naturally most pleasing parts of the female shape have I seen assume an appearance absolutely disgusting; and all from an *outré* air, vulgar manners, or hoydening postures. The bosom, which should be prominent, by a lounging attitude, sinks into slovenly flatness, rounding the back, and projecting the shoulders! On the one side, I have seen a finely-proportioned figure transform herself into a perfect fright, by this awkward neglect of all propriety and grace; and on the other, I am acquainted with a lady, whose beauty, taken in the common acceptation of the word, would not obtain her a second look, but in the elegance of her manners, in the dignity of her carriage, in the taste and disposition of her attire and in the thousand inexpressible charms which distinguish the gentlewoman, she is so powerful that none can behold her without captivation.

It is the opinion of wiser heads than mine, that no circumstance, however trifling in itself, should be neglected, which strengthens the bonds of an honourable and mutual attachment; and so great is the privilege allowed for this purpose, that it is deemed laudable in woman to collect into herself all the innocent advantages, mentally and corporeally, which may render her most admirable and precious in the eyes of him who may be, or is, her husband.

This latter sentiment reminds me to impress upon my young friends, that there are shades of demeanour which must be varied according to the sex, degree, and affinity of the persons with whom she converses. To men of all ranks and relations, she must ever hold a reserve on certain subjects, and indeed on almost every occasion, that she does not deem necessary to observe with regard to her own sex. To inferiors of both sexes she must ever preserve a gracious condescension; but to the men, a certain air of majesty must be mixed with it, that she need not assume to the women. To her equals, particularly of the male sex, her manners must never lose sight of a dignity sufficient to remind them that she expects respect will be joined with probable intimacy. In short, no intimacy should ever be so familiar as to allow of any infringement on the decent reserves which are the only preservers of refinement in friendship and love. What are called *cronies* amongst girls, are among the worst of connexions, as they generally are the very hotbeds of fancified love-fits, secrecies, and really vulgar tale-bearing.

"Celestial friendship!
Whene'er she stoops to visit earth, one shrine
The goddess finds, and one alone,
To make her sweet amends for absent Heaven,—
The bosom of a friend, where heart meets heart,
Reciprocally soft—
Each other's pillow to repose divine!"

This friendship is indeed the gift of Heaven —a boon more precious than much fine gold; but it is not usually to be found in school *cronies* or in the confidence of misses, whose unbosomings usually consist of flirtations, complaints against parents and guardians, and schemes for future parties of pleasure. Friendship is too sacred for these pretenders; under her influence, "heart meets heart," and acknowledges her as the pledge of Heaven to man, of immortality, and endless joy. To such an intimate your whole soul may be laid open. But such an intimate is rare. You may meet her once in the shape of a female friend, and in that of a tender husband! But believe not that her appearance will be more frequent. Hers are "like angels' visits, few and far between!" Earth would be too much like heaven, were it otherwise.

To the generality, then, of your equals, while you are affable and amiable with them all, you must be intimate with few, and preserve an ingenuous reserve with most. Show them your sense of propriety demands a certain distance, and with redoubled respect they will yield what you require. With men of your acquaintance, you ought to be more reserved than with women. But while I counsel such dignity of manners, you must not suppose that I mean starchness stiffness, prudery; I only recommend the mo desty of the virgin—the sober dignity of matron years.

It is to be regretted that there are not a few conceited and flippant young men, who, relying on their claims of wealth or birth, consider themselves exempted from the general obligation of deference and courtesy towards the fairer sex. Those unmannered persons are too prone to address ladies with unbecoming familiarity, to be careless in their choice of words, rude in their gestures and movements, and insolent in their unrespectful stare. The offences of such individuals in this respect are even less entitled to excuse than the ill manners of a vulgar and uneducated man, who, rising in the scale of society, finds it difficult to leave behind him the habits of early life.

Both these classes of offenders, however, are to be checked and punished, by every lady who is desirous of upholding the dignity and influence of her sex. When any man, who is not privileged by the right of friendship or of kindred to address her with an air of affection, attempts to take her hand, let her withdraw it immediately, with an air so declarative of displeasure, that he shall not presume to repeat the offence. At no time ought she to volunteer shaking hands with a male acquaintance, who holds not any particular bond of esteem with regard to herself or family. A touch, a pressure of the hands, are the only external signs a woman can give of entertaining a particular regard for certain individuals; and to lavish this valuable power of expression upon all comers, upon the impudent and contemptible, is an indelicate extravagance which, I hope, needs only to be exposed to be put for ever out of countenance.

As to the salute, the pressure of the lips—that is an interchange of affectionate greeting, or tender farewell, sacred to the dearest connexions alone. Our parents—our brothers—our near kindred—our husband—our lover, ready to become our husband,—our bosom's inmate, the friend of *our heart's core*—to them are exclusively consecrated the lips of delicacy,—and woe be to her who yields them to the stain of profanation!

By the last word, I do not mean the embrace of vice, but merely that indiscriminate facility which some young women have in permitting what they call a *good-natured kiss.* These *good-natured kisses* have often very bad effects, and can never be permitted without injuring the fine gloss of that exquisite modesty, which is the fairest garb of virgin beauty.

I remember, says a traveller, the Count M——, one of the most accomplished and handsomest young men in Vienna. When I was there, he was passionately in love with a girl of almost peerless beauty. She was the daughter of a man of great rank and influence at court; and on these considerations, as well as in regard to her charms, she was followed by a multitude of suitors. She was lively and amiable, and treated them all with an affability which still kept them in her train, although it was generally known that she had avowed a predilection for Count M——, and that preparations were making for their nuptials. The Count was of a refined mind and delicate sensibility. He loved her for herself alone—for the virtues which he believed dwelt in a beautiful form; and, like a lover of such perfections, he never approached her without timidity, and when he touched her, a fire shot through his veins that warned him not to invade the vermilion sanctuary of her lips. Such were his feelings, when one night at his intended father-in-law's, a party of young people were met to celebrate a certain festival. Several of the young lady's rejected suitors were present. Forfeits were one of the pastimes, and all went on with the greatest merriment till the Count was commanded by some witty mademoiselle to redeem his glove by saluting the cheek of his intended bride. The Count blushed, trembled, advanced to his mistress, retreated, advanced again—and at last, with a tremour that shook every fibre in his frame, with a modest grace he put the soft ringlet which played upon her cheek to his lips, and retired to demand his redeemed pledge in evident confusion. His mistress gaily smiled, and the game went on. One of her rejected suitors, but who was of a merry unthinking disposition, was adjudged, by the same indiscreet crier of the forfeits,—" as his last treat before he hanged himself," she said,—to snatch a kiss from the lips of the object of his recent vows—

" Lips whose broken sighs such fragrance fling,
As Love had fanned them freshly with his wing!"

A lively contest between the lady and the gentleman lasted for a minute; but the lady yielded, though in the midst of a convulsive laugh. And the Count had the mortification, the agony, to see the lips, which his passionate and delicate love would not allow him to touch, kissed with roughness and repetition by another man, and one whom he despised. Without a word, he rose from his chair, left the room—and the house; and, by that *good-natured kiss,* the fair boast of Vienna lost her husband and her lover. The Count never saw her more.

ON THE

MANAGEMENT OF THE PERSON IN DANCING.

On with the dance! let joy be unconfined

Childe Harold.

It is vain to expend large sums of money and large portions of time in the acquirement of accomplishments, unless some attention be also paid to the attainment of a certain grace in their exercise, which, though a circumstance distinct from themselves, is the secret of their charms and pleasure-exciting quality.

As dancing is the accomplishment most calculated to display a fine form, elegant taste, and graceful carriage, to advantage; so towards it, our regards must be particularly turned; and we shall find that when Beauty, in all her power, is to be set forth, she cannot choose a more effective exhibition.

By the *exhibition*, it must not be understood that I mean to insinuate any thing like that scenic exhibition which we may expect from professors of the art, who often, regardless of modesty, not only display the symmetry of their persons, but indelicately expose them, by most improper dresses and attitudes, on the public stage. What I propose by calling dancing an elegant mode of showing a fine form to advantage, has nothing more in it, than to teach the lovely young woman to move unembarrassed and with peculiar grace through the mazes of a dance, performed either in a private circle or public ball.

It must always be remembered, and it cannot be too often repeated, "That whatever it is worth while to do, it is worth while to do *well.*" Therefore as all times and nations have deemed dancing a salubrious, decorous, and beautiful exercise, or rather happy pastime and celebration of festivity, I cannot but regard it with particular complacency. Dancing carries with it a banquet alike for taste and feeling. The spectator of a well-ordered ball sees, at one view, in a number of elegant young women, every species of female loveliness. He beholds the perfection of personal proportion. They are attired with all the gay habiliments of fashion and of fancy; and their harmonious and agile movements unfold to him, at every turn, the ever-varying, ever-charming grace of motion.

Thus far his senses only are gratified. But the pleasure stops not there. His best feelings receive their share also. He looks on each gay countenance, he sees hilarity in every step; he listens to their delightful converse, communicated by snatches; and, with a pleasure sympathizing with theirs, he cannot but acknowledge that dancing is one of the most innocent and rational, as well as the most elegant amusements of youth

DANCING.

It is indeed the favourite pastime of nature. We find it in courts, we meet it on the village green. Here the rustic swain whispers his ardent suit to his blushing maid, while his beating heart bounds against hers in the swift wheel of the rapid dance. There the polished courtier breathes a soft sigh into the ear of the lady of his vows, as he and she timidly entwine their arms in the graceful *allemande.* But dancing has been appropriated to higher purposes than these; it formed a part of the religious ceremonies of the Jews.

In every age of fashion but the present, dancing was as much expected from young persons of both sexes, as that they should join in smiles when mutually pleased. In days of yore, in the most polite eras of Greece and Rome, and of the chivalrous ages, we find, that dancing was a favourite amusement with the first ranks of men. Kings, heroes, and unbearded youth, alike mingled in the graceful exercise.

The utmost in dancing to which a gentle woman ought to aspire, is an agile and graceful movement of her feet, an harmonious motion with her arms, and a corresponding easy carriage of her whole body. But, when she has gained this proficiency, should she find herself so unusually mistress of the art as to be able, in any way, to rival the professors by whom she has been taught, she must ever hold in mind, that *the same style of dancing is not equally proper for all kinds of dances.*

For instance, the country-dance and the cotillion, require totally different movements. I know that it is a common thing to introduce all the varieties of opera-steps into the simple figure of the former. This ill-judged fashion is inconsistent with the character of the dance, and consequently so destroys the effect, that no pleasure is produced to the eye of the judicious spectator by so discordant an exhibition. The characteristic of a country-dance is that of *gay simplicity.* The steps should be few and easy, and the corresponding motion of the arms and body unaffected, modest, and graceful.

Before I go farther upon the subject, I canno but stop a little to dwell more particularly on the necessity there is for more attention than we usually find paid to the management of the arms, and general person, in dancing.

In looking on at a ball, perhaps you will see that every woman in a dance of twenty couple, moves her feet with sufficient attention to beauty and elegance; but, with regard to the deportment of the rest of the person, most likely you will not discover one in a hundred who seems to know more about it than the most uncultivated damsel that ever jogged at a village ball.

I cannot exactly describe what it is that we see in the carriage of our young ladies in the dance; for it is difficult to point out a want by any other expression than a negative. But it is only requisite for my readers to recall to memory the many inanimate, ungraceful forms, from the waist upwards, that they nightly see at balls, and I need not describe more circumstantially.

For these ladies to suppose that they are fine dancers because they execute a variety of difficult steps with ease and precision, is a great mistake. The motion of the feet is but half the art of dancing; the other, and indeed the most conspicuous part, lies in the movement of the body, arms, and head. Here elegance must be conspicuous.

The body should always be poised with such ease as to command a power of graceful undulation, in harmony with the motion of the limbs in the dance. Nothing is more ugly than a stiff body and neck during this lively exercise. The general carriage should be elevated and light; the chest thrown out, the head easily erect, but flexible to move with every turn of the figure; and the limbs should be all braced and animated with the spirit of motion, which seems ready to bound through the very air. By this elasticity pervading the whole person when the dancer moves off, her flexible shape will gracefully sway with the varied steps of her feet; and her arms, instead of hanging loosely by her side, or rising abruptly and squarely up to take hands with her partner, will be raised in beautiful and harmonious unison and time with the music and the figure; and her whole person will thus exhibit to the delighted eye perfection in beauty, grace, and motion.

This attention to the movement of the general figure, and particularly to that of the arms (for with them is the charm of elegant action,) though, in a moderated degree, is equally applicable to the country-dance and the Scotch reel, as to the minuet, the cotillon, and other French dances.

A general idea of natural grace, in all dances, being laid down as a first principle in this elegant art, I shall suggest a few remarks on the leading characters of each style; and from them, I hope, my fair friends will be able to gather some rules which may serve them as useful auxiliaries to the lessons of their dancing-master.

The common country-dance, as its very name implies, consists of simplicity and cheerfulness; hence the female who engages in it, must aim at nothing more, in treading its easy mazes, than executing a few simple steps with unaffected elegance. Her body, her arms, the turn of her head, the expression of her countenance, all must bear the same character of negligent grace, of elegant activity, of decorous gaiety.

The Scotch reel has steps appropriated to itself, and in the dance can never be displaced for those of France, without an absurdity too ridiculous even to imagine without laughing. There are no dancers in the world more expressive of inward hilarity and happiness than the Scotch are, when performing in their own reels. The music is sufficient—so jocund are its sounds—to set a whole company on their feet in a moment, and to dance with all their might, till it ceases, like people bit by the tarantula. Hence, as the character of reels is merriment, they must be performed with much more *joyance* of manner than even the country-dance; and, therefore, they are better adapted, as society is now constituted to the social private circle than to the public ball. They demand a frankness of deportment, an undisguised jocularity, which few large parties will properly admit; therefore, they are more at home in the baronial and kindred-filled hall of the thane of the Highland clan, than in the splendid and mixed ball-room of the modish man of fashion.

French dances, which include minuets, cotillons, and all the round of *ballet* figures, admit of every new refinement and dexterity in the agile art; and, while exhibiting in them, there is no step, no turn, no attitude, within the verge of maiden delicacy, that the dancer may not adopt and practise.

Though much of graceful display is made in these dances, yet there are many rivals in the cotillon contending for the palm of superiority; and the contest, throughout, if maintained with the original elegant decorum of the design, may be continued with undeviating modesty and discretion.

But with regard to the lately introduced German waltz, I cannot speak so favourably; I must agree with Goethé, when writing of the national dance of his country, " that none but husbands and wives can with any propriety be partners in the waltz."

There is something in the close approximation of persons, in the attitudes, and in the motion, which ill agrees with the delicacy of woman, should she be placed in such a situation with any other man than the most intimate connexion she can have in life. Indeed, I have often heard men, of no very-overstrained feeling, say "that there are very few women in the world with whom they could bear to dance the German waltz."

The fandango, though graceful in its own ountry—because danced, from custom, with as reserved a mind as our maidens would make a curtsey,—is, nevertheless, when attempted here, too great a display of the person for any modest American woman to venture. It is a *solo!* Imagine what must be the assurance of the young woman, who, unaccustomed by the habits of her country to such singular exhibitions of herself, could get up in a room full of company, and, with an unblushing face, go through all the evolutions, postures, and vaultings, of the Spanish fandango? Certainly, there are few discreet men in our country who would say, "such a woman I should like for my wife!"

The castanets, which are used in this dance, by attracting extraordinary attention, afford an ther argument against its being adopted anywhere but on the stage. The tambourin, the cymbals, and all other noisy accompaniments, in the hands of a lady-dancer, are equally blameable; and though a woman may, by their means, exhibit her agility and person to advantage, she may depend on it, that while the artist only is admired, the woman will sink into contempt; and that, though she may possibly meet with lovers to throw a score of embroidered handkerchiefs at her feet, she will hardly encounter one of a thousand who will venture to trust himself to the offering her the bond of a single gold ring.

The bullero, another of our Spanish importations, is a dance of so questionable a description, that I cannot but proscribe it also. It may be performed with perfect modesty; but the sentiment of it depends so entirely on the disposition of the dancer, that Delicacy dare hardly venture to enrol herself in its lists, lest the partner chosen for her might be of a temper to turn its gaiety into licentiousness; to produce blushes of shame where she promised herself the glow of pleasure, and send her away from what ought to have been an innocent amusement, filled with the bitterness of insulted delicacy.

In short, in addressing my fair countrywomen on this subject, I would sum up my advice, in regard to the choice of dances, by warning them against the introduction of new-fangled fashions of this sort. Let them leave the languishing and meretricious attitudes of modern *ballet*-teachers to the dancing-girls of India, or to the Circassian slaves of Turkey, whose disgraceful business is to please a tyrant for whom they can feel no love.

Let our American fair also turn away from the almost equally unchaste dances of the southern kingdoms of Europe, and, content with the gay step of France, and the active merriments of England and Scotland, with their own festive movements, continue their native country balls to their blameless delight, and to the gratification of every tasteful and benevolent observer.

While thus remarking on the manner of dancing, it may not be unacceptable to add a few words on the dress most appropriate to its light and unembarrassed motion.

Long trains are, of course, too cumbrous an appendage to be intentionally assumed when proposing to dance; but it must also be remarked, that very short petticoats are as inelegant as the others are inconvenient. Scanty circumscribed habiliments impede the action of the limbs, and, besides their indelicacy, show the leg in the least graceful of all possible points of view. The most elegant attire for a ball is, that the under garments should be absolutely short, but the upper one, which should be of light material, should reach at least to the top of the instep. It should also be sufficiently full to fall easily in folds from the waist downwards to the foot. By this arrangement, when the dancer begins her graceful exercise, the drapery will elegantly adapt itself to the motion and contour of her limbs; and falling accidentally on her foot, or as accidentally when she bounds along, discovering, under its flying folds, her beautifully-turned ankle. Symmetry and grace will be occasionally displayed, almost unconsciously, and thus Modesty, taken unawares, will adorn, with her blushes, the perfect lineaments of female beauty.

MANAGEMENT OF THE PERSON

IN SINGING, PLAYING ON THE PIANO-FORTE, HARP, &c.

WHAT has been said in behalf of simple and appropriate dancing, may also be whispered in the ear of the fair practitioner in music; and, by analogy, she may, not unbeneficially, apply the suggestions to her own case.

There are many young women, who when they sit down to the piano or the harp, or to sing, twist themselves into so many contortions, and writhe their bodies and faces about into such actions and grimaces, as would almost incline one to believe that they are suffering under the torture of the toothache or the gout. Their bosoms heave, their shoulders shrug, their heads swing to the right and left, their lips quiver, their eyes roll; they sigh, they pant, they seem ready to expire! And what is all this about? They are merely playing a favourite concerto, or singing a new Italian song.

If it were possible for these conceit-intoxicated warblers, these languishing dolls, to guess what rational spectators say of their follies, they would be ready to break their instruments and be dumb for ever. What they call *expression in singing*, at the rate they would show it, is only fit to be exhibited on the stage, when the character of the song intends to portray the utmost ecstasy of passion to a sighing swain. In short, such an echo to the words and music of a love-ditty, is very improper in any young woman who would wish to be thought as pure in heart as in person. If amatory addresses are to be sung, let the expression be in the voice and the composition of the air, not in the looks and gestures of the lady-singer. The utmost that she ought to allow herself to do, when thus breathing out the accents of love, is to wear a serious, tender countenance. More than this is bad, and may produce reflections in the minds of the hearers very inimical to the reputation of he fair warbler.

By this slight sketch, my fair readers will perceive that I mean *simplicity* to be the principle and the decoration of all their actions; as it should pervade them in the dance, so it should imbue their voice and action in playing and in singing.

Let their attitude at the piano or the harp be easy and graceful. I strongly exhort them to avoid a stiff, awkward, elbowing position at either; they must observe an elegant flow of figure at both. The latter certainly admits of most grace, as the shape of the instrument is calculated, in every respect, to show a fine figure to advantage. The contour of the whole form, the turn and polish of a beautiful hand and arm, the richly-slippered and well-made foot on the pedal stops, the gentle motion of a lovely neck, and, above all, the sweetly-tempered expression of an intelligent countenance; these are shown at one glance when the fair performer is seated unaffectedly, yet gracefully, at the harp.

Similar beauty of position may be seen in a lady's management of a lute, a guitar, a mandolin, or a lyre. The attitude at a piano-forte or at a harpsichord, is not so happily adapted to grace. From the shape of the instrument, the performer must sit directly in front of a straight line of keys; and her own posture being correspondingly erect and square, it is hardly possible that it should not appear rather inelegant. But if it attain not the *ne plus ultra* of grace, at least she may prevent an air of stiffness; she may move her hands easily on the keys, and bear her head with that elegance of carriage which cannot fail to impart its own character to the whole of her figure. One of the most graceful forms that I ever saw sit at an instrument, is that of St. Cecilia, painted by Sir Joshua Reynolds, playing on the organ. It is the portrait of the late Mrs. R. B. Sheridan; and, from the simplicity of the attitude, and the graceful elevation of the head, it is, without exception, one of the most interesting pictures I ever beheld.

If ladies, in meditating on grace of deportment, would rather consult the statues of fine sculptors, and the figures of excellent painters, than the lessons of their dancing-masters, or the dictates of their looking-glasses, we should, doubtless, see simplicity where we now find affectation, and a thousand ineffable graces taking place of the present *régime* of absurdity and conceit.

It was by studying the perfect sculpture of Greece and Rome, that a certain lady of rank, eminent for her peculiarly beautiful attitudes, acquired so great a superiority in mien above her fair contemporaries of every court in which she became an inmate. It was by meditating on the classic pictures of Poussin, that one of the first tragic actresses on the French stage learnt to move and look like the *daughter of the sun.* And by a similar study, did Mrs. Siddons derive inspiration from the pencil of Corregio and Rubens.

MANAGEMENT OF THE PERSON

IN DRAWING, READING, &c

Glancing at the graphic art, reminds me that some degree of proficiency in this interesting accomplishment is also an object of study with my fair young countrywomen. I shall not make any observation on their progress in the art itself, but only with regard to their manner of practising it.

Both for health and beauty's sake, they should be careful not to stoop too much, or to sit too long in the exercise of the pencil. A bending position of the chest and head, when frequently assumed, is apt to contract the lungs, round the back, redden the face, and give painful digestions and headach. An awkward posture in writing, reading, or sewing, is productive of the same bad effects; and, what may seem almost incredible, (but many who have witnessed the same, can, I am sure, give their evidence in support of my representation,) there are young persons, who, when writing, drawing, reading, or working, keep a sort of ludicrous time with their occupations, by making a succession of unmeaning and hideous grimaces. I have seen a pretty young woman, while writing a letter to her lover, draw up her lips, and twist the muscles of her face in every direction that her pen moved; and so ugly did she look during this sympathetic performance, that I could not forbear thinking that, could her swain see the object then dictating her vows, he would take fright at the metamorphosis, and never be made to believe it could be the same person.

Mumbling to yourself, while reading, is also another very inelegant habit. A person should either read determinately so much aloud as to be heard distinctly by the company present, or peruse her book without even moving her lips. An inward muttering, or a silent motion of the mouth, while reading, is equally unpleasant to the observer, and disfiguring to the observed.

In short, there is nothing, however minute in manners, however insignificant in appearance that does not demand some portion of attention from a well-bred and highly-polished young woman. An author of no small literary renown, has observed, that several of the minutest habits or acts of some individuals may give sufficient reasons to guess at their temper. The choice of a gown, or even the folding and sealing of a letter, will bespeak the shrew and the scold, the careless and the negligent.

MANAGEMENT OF THE VOICE;

CONSISTENCY OF

DEPORTMENT AND DRESS

THE manner of speech is important. The very voice of an individual, the tone she assumes in speaking to strangers, or even familiarly to her friends, will lead a keen observer to discover what elements her temper is made of. The low key belongs to the sullen, sulky, obstinate; the shrill note to the petulant, the pert, the impatient: some will pronounce the common and trite question "how *do* you *do?*" with such harshness and asperity, that they seem positively angry with you that you should ever *do* at all. Some affect a lisping, which at once betrays childishness and downright nonsense; others will bid their words gallop so swiftly, that the ablest ear is unable to follow the rapid race, and gathers nothing but confused and unmeaning sounds. All these extremes are to be avoided and, although nature has differently formed the organs of speech for different individuals, yet there is a mode to correct nature's own aberrations. I have heard of sensible men, who, merely for the tone of voice which did not quite harmonize with their ears, have dropped their connexion with women, who, in all other points were unexceptionable.

Admit this, and another salutary truth will be made manifest. If good-breeding and graceful refinement are ever *most proper*, they are always so. It is not sufficient that Amaryllis is amiable and elegant in her whole deportment to strangers and to her acquaintance; she must be undeviatingly so to her most intimate friends to nearest relations, to father, mother, brothers, sisters, husband. She must have no *dishabille* for them, either of mind or person.

This last word inclines me to pursue the hint farther; to exhort my fair readers, while I plead for consistency in manners, also to carry the analogy to dress. If they would always appear amiable, elegant, and endearing to the beings with whom they are to spend their lives, let them always make those beings the first objects for whose pleasure their accomplishments, their manners, and their dress are to be cultivated. Let them never appear before these tender relatives in the disgusting negligence of disordered and soiled clothes. By this has many a lovely girl lost her lover; and by this has many an amiable wife alienated the affections of her husband.

Let me, then, in concluding this chapter, again repeat, that consistency is the soul of female power, the charm of her fascination, the bond of her social happiness.

DIGNITY AND FAMILIARITY

OF

DEPORTMENT.

The carriage of a woman to her equals being founded on a just appreciation of their merits, and a proper respect to herself, the same sentiment will be found to pervade her conduct to her superiors in rank.

With regard to men, when they occupy a higher station than herself, she must proportion reverential courtesy to them according to the rules of ceremony. If she knows them merely as officers high in authority, her manner must then be that of calm, dignified respect. But when she finds that merit is yet higher in any of these men than his tit.es, then, let her show the homage of the soul, as well as that of the body; for real greatness ennobles the head which bows.

We regard society as a grand machine, in which each member has the place best fitted for him; or, to make use of a more common illustration, as a vast drama, in which every person has the part allotted to him most appropriate to his abilities. One enacts the general, others the subalterns, others the soldiery; but all obey the Great Director, who best knows what is in man. Regarding things in this light, all arrogance, all pride, all envyings and contempt of others, from their relative degrees, disappear, as emotions to which we have no pretensions. We neither endowed ourselves with high birth nor eminent talents. We are altogether beings of a creation independent of our own will; and, therefore, bearing our own honours as a gift, not as a right, we should condescend to our inferiors (whose place it might have been our lot to fill,) and regard with deference our superiors, whom

Heaven, by so elevating, has intended that we should respect.

This sentiment of order in the mind, this conviction of the beautiful harmony in a well-organized, civil society, gives us dignity with our inferiors, without alloying it with the smallest particle of pride; by keeping them at a due distance, we merely maintain ourselves and them in the rank in which a higher Power has placed us; and the condescension of our general manners to them, and our kindnesses in their exigencies, and generous approbation of their worth, are sufficient acknowledgements of sympathy, to show that we avow the same nature with themselves, the same origin, the same probation, the same end.

Our demeanour with our equals is more a matter of policy. To be indiscreetly familiar, to allow of liberties being taken with your good-nature, all this is likely to happen with people of the same rank with ourselves, unless we hold our mere acquaintance at a proper distance, by a certain reserve. A woman may be gay, ingenuous, perfectly amiable to her associates, and yet reserved. Avoid all sudden intimacies, all needless secret-telling, all closeting about nonsense, caballing, taking mutual liberties with each other in regard to domestic arrangements; in short, beware of familiarity! The kind of familiarity which is common in families, and amongst women of the same classes in society, is that of an indiscriminate gossiping; an interchange of thoughts without any effusion of the heart. Then an unceremonious way of reproaching each other, for a real or supposed neglect; a coarse manner of declaring your faults; a habit of jangling on trifles; a habit of preferring your own whims or ease before that of the persons about you; an indelicate way of breaking into each other's privacy. In short, doing every thing that declares the total oblivion of all politeness and decent manners.

This series of errors happens every day amongst brothers and sisters, husbands and wives, and female acquaintances; and what are the consequences? Distaste, disgust, everlasting quarrels, and perhaps total estrangement in the end!

I have seen many families bound together by the tenderest affection; I have seen many hearts wrought into each other by the sweet amalgamation of friendship; but with none did I ever find this delicious foretaste of the society in Elysium, where a never-failing politeness was not mingled in all their thoughts, words, and actions, to each other.

CONCLUSION

"Can comeliness of form, or shape, or air,
With comeliness of words or deeds compare?
No! those at first th' unwary heart may gain,
But these, these only, can the heart retain."

GAY

WHEN so much has been said of the body and its accoutrements, I cannot but subjoin a few words on the intelligence which animates the frame, and of the organ which imparts its meaning.

Connected speech is granted to mankind alone. Parrots may prate, and monkeys chatter, but it is only to the reasonable being that power of combining ideas, expressing their import, and uttering in audible sounds, in all its various gradations, the language of sense and judgment, of love and resentment, is awarded as a gift, that gives us a proud and undeniable superiority to all the rest of the creation.

To employ this faculty well and gracefully, is one grand object of education. The mere organ itself, as to sound, is like a musical instrument, to be modulated with elegance, or struck with the disorderly nerve of coarseness and vulgarity.

I must add to what has been said before on the subject, that excessive rapidity of speaking is, in general, even with a clear enunciation, very disagreeable; but, when it is accompanied with a shrill voice, the effect is inexpressibly discordant and hideous. The first orator the heathen world ever knew, so far remedied the natural defects of his speech, (and they were most embarrassing,) as to become the most easy and persuasive of speakers. In like manner, when a young woman finds any difficulty or inelegance in her speech, she ought to pay the strictest attention to rectify the fault.

Should she have too quick or encumbeied an articulation, she ought to read with extreme slowness for several hours in the day, and even pay attention, in speaking, to check the rapidity or confusion of her utterance. By similar antidota, means, she must attack a propensity of talking in a high key. Better err in the opposite extreme while she is prosecuting her cure, as the voice will gradually and imperceptibly attain its most harmonious pitch, than by at first attempting the medium, most likely retain too much of the screaming key. A clear articulation, a tempered intonation, and in a moderate key, are essentials in the voice of an accomplished female. Her graceful peculiarities must be the gift of nature, or the effect of cultivated taste. Fine judgment and delicate sensibility are the best schoolmistresses on this subject. Indeed, where, in relation to man or woman, shall we find that an improved understanding, an enlightened mind, and a refined taste, are not the best polishers of manners, and in all respects the most efficient handmaids of the Muses?

Let me, then, in one short sentence, in one tender adieu, my fair readers and endeared friends! enforce upon your minds, that if Beauty be woman's weapon, it must be feathered by the Graces, pointed by the eye of Discretion, and shot by the hand of Virtue!

Look, then, not merely to your mirrors, when you would decorate yourselves for conquest, but consult the *speculum*, which will reflect your hearts and minds. Remember that it is the affections of a sensible and reasonable soul you hope to subdue, and seek for arms likely to carry the fortress.

He that is worthy, must love corresponding excellence. Which of you all would wish to marry a man merely for the colour of his eye, or the shape of his leg? Think not then worse of him than you would do of yourselves; and hope not to satisfy his better wishes with the possession of a merely handsome wife.

Beauty of person will ever be found a dead letter, unless it be animated with beauty of mind. "For 't is the mind that makes the body rich." We must, then, not only cultivate the shape, the complexion, the air, the attire, the manners, but most assiduously must our attention be devoted to teach "the young idea how to shoot," and to fashion the unfolding mind to judgment and virtue. By such culture, it will not be merely the charming girl, the captivating woman we shall present to the world, but the dutiful daughter, affectionate sister, tender wife, judicious mother, faithful friend, and amiable acquaintance.

The cultivation of the intellectual powers, so necessary to the full development of the female mind, requires some attention to the choice of suitable books—those which will at the same time store the memory with rich subjects for conversation, and embellish the taste. If I were to hazard a few words of advice on this subject, I would recommend to my fair readers to furnish their libraries with a copy of the far-famed Encyclopædia Americana, as a solid foundation of natural and moral science, history, and biography,—an excellent book of reference on any subject of information in which one may feel deficient, or may desire to refresh the memory. Its excellence in furnishing materials for intelligent conversation, is universally acknowledged.

To form the taste by an unquestionable model of style in English composition, one should read the works of our American Addison, the elegant author of the Sketch-Book. All that Johnson has said in favour of the renowned "Spectator" may with greater force and justice be applied to Irving.

If a lady finds some time at her disposal which may safely be devoted to fiction, the works of

Cooper, Bird, and Kennedy among our own countrymen, and those of Walter Scott, Mr. Dickens, Miss Austen, the Misses Porter, Miss Mitford and Miss Edgeworth among the British novelists, should be placed highest on the list.

In biography, the lives of Walter Scott, Crabbe, Cabot, Cardinal Richelieu, and Cardinal De Retz may serve as an introduction. The biographical notices of statesmen and the illustrious characters of our own country in the Encyclopædia Americana, having been furnished by Mr. Walsh, will be found complete and accurate.

In poetry, after the standard poets of the last century of whose works a sufficient quantity is comprised in Dr. Aikin's collection, one should read Scott, portions of Byron, all of Crabbe, Joanna Baillie, Wordsworth, Hemans, and Coleridge.

Much of the history of our own country may be gleaned by a careful perusal of the different articles in the Encyclopædia, coming under this head. Mackintosh's History of England, Scott's History of Scotland, Grattan's of the Netherlands, Crowe's of France, Sismondi's of Italy, and the histories of Spain and Portugal, and of Rome, comprised in the Cabinet Cyclopædia, will, with the articles on foreign history in the Encyclopædia Americana, to which we have already so frequently referred, furnish one with ample means of intelligence in this useful and important branch of liberal education.

The Works of Lady Mary Wortley Montague are also entitled to attention. Lady Montague's celebrity as an epistolary writer is unsurpassed, and her descriptions of the countries she visited are very lively, striking, and graphic. She is justly considered one of the best writers of the famous age of Queen Anne.

Murray's Encyclopædia of Geography is another very important work. This is the completest view of the world, in its physical, statistical, and moral relations, which has yet appeared. It occupies three imperial octavo volumes, and contains more than a thousand illustrations from original drawings, relating to the manners and customs, animal, vegetable, and mineral productions, and towns, cities, and famous buildings in the world

The Book of Flowers, and the Language of Flowers, are elegant trifles, suited to a lady's boudoir.

Miss Austen's novels may be recommended for their quiet, domestic scenes, their uniform purity of sentiment and naturalness of character. Lady Morgan's are valuable for the light they throw upon continental as well as English and Irish life and manners, and their fearless advocacy of liberal principles in politics.

I might extend this list further, and go into every department of knowledge; but in a work like the present, I may be deemed to have transcended the boundaries of my subject, by naming the works which first occurred to me as most suitable for a lady's reading; but the judicious reader will hardly consider it impertinent in me, to mention my favourite books, when insisting on the importance of intellectual cultivation to the perfecting of female beauty. So long as the highest degree of beauty shall consist in the expression of soul, feeling and intelligence in happy union, so long it will be important for a lady to be careful in the selection of her books.

APPENDIX.

APPENDIX.

ON THE USE OF CORSETS.

FASHION lives on novelty, and we have on this account much charity for its wanderings and eccentricities. Bonnets, with a snout as long as an elephant's proboscis, or a margin as broad as a bushel measure, are merely ridiculous. Shoulders that look like wings, and sleeves as wide as a petticoat, we think are not particularly graceful; but they have at least the merit of being airy, and we take no offence. We cannot, however, extend our indulgence to the compressed waist which is the rage at present. We know that as often as the waist is lengthened to its natural limits, this tendency to abridge its diameter appears; and we confess we are puzzled to account for the fact; for surely it is strange, that a permanent prepossession should exist in favour of a mode of dress which is at once ugly, unnatural, and pernicious. Were fashion under the guidance of taste, the principles of drapery in painting and sculpture would never be lost sight of in its changes. The clothes that cover us may be disposed in an infinite variety of forms, without violating those rules which the artist is careful to observe. The true form of the body ought to be disclosed to the eye, without the shape being exhibited in all its minutiæ, as in the dress of a harlequin; but in no case should the natural proportions (supposing the figure to be good) be changed. Ask the sculptor what he thinks of a fashionable waist, pinched till it rivals the lady's neck in tenuity, and he will tell you it is monstrous. Consult the physician, and you will learn that this is one of those follies in which no female can long indulge with impunity; for health, and even life, are often sacrificed to it.

Corsets are used partly as a warm covering to the chest, and partly to furnish a convenient attachment to other parts of the female dress. This is all proper and correct; but to these uses fashion superadds others, originating in fantastical notions of beauty. Corsets are employed to modify the shape, to render the chest as small below, and as broad above, as possible, and to increase the elevation, fulness, and prominence of the bosom. To show how this affects the condition of the body, we must begin by giving a short description of the thorax or chest, which is the subject of this artificial compression.

Every one who has seen a skeleton, knows that the chest consists of a cavity protected by a curious frame-work of bones. These are, 1st, the back-bone, (consisting of *vertebræ*, or short bones jointed into one another) which sustains the whole upper part of the trunk; 2d, the breast-bone, about seven or eight inches long, and composed of three pieces; and 3dly, the ribs, of which there are generally twenty-four. The twelve ribs on each side are all fixed to the back-bone behind; seven of these, the seven uppermost, are also attached to the breast-bone before, and are, therefore, called *true ribs.* The eighth rib has its end turned up, and rests on the seventh; the ninth rests in the same way on the eighth; but the tenth, eleventh, and twelfth are not connected with one another in front at all. The fore extremity of each rib consists not of bone, but of an elastic substance called cartilage. The elasticity of this substance combined with the oblique position of the ribs, constitutes a beautiful provision, in consequence of which the chest enlarges and contracts its volume to afford free play to the lungs.

We now wish to call attention to the form f this cavity, which, as we have seen, is surrounded and protected by the back-bone, ribs, and breast-bone, and is called the *thorax*, or chest. The uppermost pair of ribs, which lie just at the bottom of the neck, are very short; the next pair is rather longer; the third longer still; and thus they go on increasing in length to the seventh pair, or last *true* ribs, after which the length diminishes, but without materially contracting the size of the cavity, because the false ribs only go round a part of the body. Hence the chest has a sort of conical shape, or it may be compared to a bee-hive as it is sometimes made, the narrow or pointed end being next the neck, and the broad end undermost. The natural form of the thorax, in short, is just the reverse of the fashionable shape of the waist. The latter is narrow below, and wide above; the former is narrow above, and wide below.

The lower part of the thorax is also much more compressible, and of course more easily injured by ligatures than the upper. In the upper part, the bones form a complete circle; and, from the small obliquity of the ribs, this circle presents a great power of resistance to external pressure. But the last five ribs, called the false ribs, besides being placed more obliquely, become weaker as they decrease in length, and having no support in front, their power of resisting external pressure is probably six times less than that of the true ribs. Hence ligatures applied to this part of the body may contract the natural size of the cavity perhaps one half. Nature, in this instance, has intrusted the belle with a discretionary power, guarding against its abuse, however, by severe penalties. If she chooses to *brave the consequences*, she may always, with the help of lace and cord, produce a great change on this part of her person.

From the great care nature has bestowed to strengthen the outer shell of the thorax, and to combine mobility with strength, we may judge of the importance of the organs within, and of the value of free motion to their healthy action. It is a further proof of this, as Soemmerring observes, that the ribs are the first part of the bony frame-work which nature forms. The thorax contains,—first, the heart, which is the centre of the circulating system, and which, for the sake of its metaphorical offices, every lady must be anxious to keep from injury;—next, the lungs which occupy by far the largest space, and of the delicacy of whose operations, every one may judge. There are, besides, either within the thorax, or in juxtaposition with it, the stomach, liver, and kidneys, with the æsophagus, the trachea, or wind-pipe, part of the intestines and many nerves, all intimately connected with the vital powers. Most of these organs are not only of primary importance in themselves, but, through the nerves, arteries, &c., their influence extends to the head, and the remotest parts of the limbs, so that when they are injured, *health is poisoned at its source*, and the mischief always travels to other parts of the body, disarranging and enfeebling the entire system, throughout all its ramifications.

Imagine, now, what is the consequence of applying compression, by corsets of some unyielding material, to a cavity enclosing so many delicate organs, whose free action is essential to health. First, the lowest part of the shell of the thorax yields most; the false ribs, and the lower true ribs, are pressed inwards; the whole viscera in this part of the body, including part of the intestines, are squeezed close together and forced upwards; and, as the pressure is continued above, they are forced higher still. If the lacing is carried farther, the breast-bone is raised, and sometimes bent; the collar-bone protrudes its inner extremity; and the shoulder-blades are forced backwards. The under part of the lungs is pressed together, and the entrance of the blood into it hindered; the abdominal viscera, being least protected, suffer severely; the stomach is compressed, its distension prevented, and its situation and form changed, giving rise to imperfect digestion; the blood is forced up to the head, where it generates various complaints; the liver has its shape altered, and its functions obstructed; the bones having their natural motion constrained, distortion ensues, and the high shoulder, the twisted spine or breastbone, begins at last to manifest itself through the integuments and the clothes.

Another highly injurious effect of tight corsets is, that those who have been long so closely laced, become at last unable to hold themselves erect, or move with comfort without them, but, as is very justly said, *fall together*, in consequence of the natural form and position of the ribs being altered. The muscles of the back are weakened and crippled, and cannot maintain themselves in their natural position for any length of time. The spine, too, no longer accustomed to bear the destined weight of the body, bends and sinks down. Where tight lacing is practised, young women, from fifteen to twenty years of age, are found so dependent upon their corsets, that they faint whenever they lay them aside, and therefore are obliged to have themselves laced before going to sleep. For as soon as the thorax and abdomen are relaxed, by being deprived of their usual support, the blood rushing downwards, in consequence of the diminished resistance to its motion, empties the vessels of the head, and thus occasions fainting.

"From 1760 to about 1770," says Soemmerring, "it was the fashion in Berlin and other parts of Germany, and also in Holland a few years ago, to apply corsets to children. This practice fell into disuse, in consequence of its being observed, that children who did not wear corsets grew up straight, while those who were treated with this extraordinary care, got by it a high shoulder or a hunch. Many families might be named, in which parental fondness selected the handsomest of several boys to put in corsets, and the result was, that these alone were hunched. The deformity was attributed at first to the improper mode of applying the corsets, till it was discovered that no child thus invested grew up straight, not to mention the risk of consumption and rupture which were likewise incurred by using them. I, for my part affirm, that I do not know any woman, who, by tight lacing, (that is, by artificial means,) has obtained 'a fine figure,' in whom I could not, by accurate examination, point out either a high shoulder, oblique compressed ribs, a lateral incurvation of the spine in the form of an italic *S*, or some other distortion. I have had opportunities of verifying this opinion among ladies of high condition, who, as models of fine form, were brought forward for the purpose of putting me to silence."

Young ladies in course of time hope to become wives, and wives to become mothers. Even in this last stage, few females have the courage to resist a practice which is in general use, though to them it is trebly injurious. But it is sufficient to glance at this branch of the subject, on which, for obvious reasons, we cannot follow our medical instructor. It is lamentable, however, that mothers who have themselves experienced the bitter fruits of tight lacing, still permit their daughters to indulge in it. There is, in truth, no tyranny like the tyranny of fashion. "I have found mothers of discernment and experience," says Soemmerring, "who predicted that in their 25th year, a hunch would inevitably be the lot of their daughters, whom they nevertheless allowed to wear corsets, because they were afraid to make their children singular."

But it is time to speak of the diseases produced by the passion for *slender waists*. "One is astonished," says Soemmerring, "at the number of diseases which corsets occasion. Those I have subjoined rest on the authority of the most eminent physicians. Tight lacing produces—

Headach, giddiness, tendency to fainting, pain in the eyes, pain and ringing in the ears, bleeding at the nose, shortness of breath, spitting of blood, consumption, derangement of the circulation, palpitation of the heart, water in the chest, loss of appetite, squeamishness, eructations, vomiting of blood, depraved digestion, flatulence, diarrhœa, colic pains, induration of the liver, dropsy and rupture. It is also followed by melancholy, hysteria, and many diseases peculiar to the female constitution, which it is not necessary to enumerate in detail."

But the injury does not fall merely on the inward structure of the body, but also on its outward beauty, and on the temper and feelings with which that beauty is associated. Beauty is in reality but another name for that expression of countenance which is the index of sound health, intelligence, good feelings, and peace of mind. All are aware, that uneasy feelings existing habitually in the breast, speedily exhibit their signature on the countenance, and that bitter thoughts, or a bad temper, spoil the human face divine of its grace. But it is not so generally known that irksome or painful sensations, though merely of a physical nature, by a law equally certain, rob the temper of its sweetness, and, as a consequence, the countenance of the more ethereal and better part of its beauty. Pope attributes the rudeness of a person usually bland and polished, to the circumstance, that "he had not dined;" in other words, his stomach was in bad order. But there are many other physical pains besides hunger that sour the temper; and, for our part, if we found ourselves sitting at dinner with a man whose body was girt on all sides by board and bone, like the north pole by thick-ribbed ice, we should no more expect to find grace, politeness, amenity, vivacity, and good-humour, in such a companion, than in Prometheus with a vulture battening on his vitals, or in Cerberus, whose task is to grow all day long in his chains.

RECIPES.

Paste of Palermo.

THIS paste for the hands, to use instead of soap, preserves them from chopping, smoothes their surface, and renders them soft.

Take a pound of soft soap, half a pint of salad oil, the same quantity of spirits of wine, the juice of three lemons, a little silver sand, and a sufficient quantity of what perfume pleases the sense. The oil and soap must be first boiled together in an earthen pipkin. The other ingredients to be added after boiling; and, when cool, amalgamate into a paste with the hands.

Fard.

This useful paste is good for taking off sunburnings, effects of weather on the face, and accidental cutaneous eruptions. It must be applied at going to bed. First wash the face with its usual ablution, and when dry, rub this fard all over it, and go to rest with it on the skin. This is excellent for almost constant use. Take two ounces of oil of sweet almonds, ditto of spermaceti; melt them in a pipkin over a slow fire. When they are dissolved and mixed, take it off the fire, and stir into it one table-spoonful of fine honey. Continue stirring it till it is cold, and then it is fit for use.

Lip Salve.

A quarter of a pound of hard marrow from the marrow-bone. Melt it over a slow fire; as it dissolves gradually, pour the liquid marrow into an earthern pipkin; then add to it an ounce of spermaceti, twenty raisins of the sun, stoned, and a small portion of alcanna root, sufficient to colour it to a bright vermilion. Simmer these ingredients over a slow fire for ten minutes, then strain the whole through muslin; and while hot, stir into it one teaspoonful of the balsam of Peru. Pour it into the boxes in which it is to remain; it will there stiffen, and become fit for use.

Lavender Water.

Take of rectified spirits of wine half a pint, essential oil of lavender two drachms, ottar of roses five drops. Mix all together in a bottle, and cork it for use.

Unction de Maintenon.

The use of this is to remove freckles. The mode of application is this:—Wash the face at night with elder-flower water, then anoint it with the unction. In the morning cleanse your skin from its oily adhesion, by washing it copiously in rose-water.

Take of Venice soap an ounce, dissolve it in half an ounce of lemon-juice, to which add of oil of bitter almonds and deliquidated oil of tar-

tar, each a quarter of an ounce. Let the mixture be placed in the sun till it acquires the consistence of ointment. When in this state, add three drops of the oil of rhodium, and keep it for use.

Creme de l'Enclos.

This is an excellent wash, to be used night and morning for the removal of tan.

Take half a pint of milk, with the juice of a lemon, and a spoonful of white brandy, boil the whole, and skim it clear from all scum. When cool, it is ready for use.

Pommade de Seville.

This simple application is much in request with the Spanish ladies, for taking off the effects of the sun, and to render the complexion brilliant.

Take equal parts of lemon-juice and white of eggs. Beat the whole together in a varnished earthen pipkin, and set on a slow fire. Stir the fluid with a wooden spoon till it has acquired the consistence of soft pomatum. Perfume it with some sweet essence, and before you apply it, carefully wash the face with rice water.

Beaume à l'Antique.

This is a very fine cure for chopped lips. Take four ounces of the oil of roses, half an ounce of white wax, and half an onnce of spermaceti, melt them in a glass vessel, and stir them with a wooden spoon; pour it out into glass cups for use.

Wash for the Hair.

This is a cleanser and brightener of the head and hair, and should be applied in the morning.

Beat up the whites of six eggs into a froth, and with that anoint the head close to the roots of the hair. Leave it to dry on; then wash the head and hair thoroughly with a mixture of rum and rose-water in equal quantities.

Aura and Cephalus.

This curious recipe is of Grecian origin, as its name plainly indicates, and is said to have been very efficacious in preventing, or even removing premature wrinkles from the face of the Athenian fair.

Put some powder of the best myrrh upon an iron plate, sufficiently heated to melt the gum gently, and when it liquifies, hold your face over it, at a proper distance to receive the fumes without inconvenience; and that you may reap the whole benefit of the fumigation, cover your head with a napkin. It must be observed, however, that if the applicant feels any headach, she must desist, as the remedy will not suit her constitution, and ill consequences might possibly ensue.

Madame Recamier's Pommade.

This was communicated by this lady as being used in France and Italy, by those who professionally, or by choice, are engaged in exercises which require long and great exertions of the limbs, as dancing, playing on instruments, &c.

Take any suitable quantity of *Axungia Cervi* i. e. the fat of a red stag or hart; add to it the same quantity of olive oil, (Florence oil is preferable to any of the kind,) and half the quantity of virgin wax; melt the whole in an earthen vessel, well glazed, over a slow fire, and, when properly mixed, leave it to cool.—This ointment has been applied also with considerable efficacy in cases of rheumatism.

A Wash for the Face.

This recipe is well known in France, and much extolled by the ladies of that country, as efficacious and harmless.

Take equal parts of the seeds of the melon pompion, gourd, and cucumber, pounded and reduced to powder or meal; add to it fresh cream sufficient to dilute the flour; beat all up together, adding a sufficient quantity of milk, as it may be required, to make an ointment, and then apply it to the face; leave it there for half an hour, and then wash it off with warm water.

A Paste for the Skin.

This may be recommended in cases when the skin seems to get too loosely attached to the muscles.

Boil the whites of four eggs in rose water, add to it a sufficient quantity of alum; beat the whole together till it takes the consistence of a paste. This will give, when applied, great firmness to the skin.

A Wash to give lustre to the Face.

Infuse wheat bran well sifted, for three or four hours in white wine vinegar; add to it five yolks of eggs and a grain or two of ambergris, and distil the whole. When the bottle is carefully corked, keep it for twelve or fifteen days before you make use of it.

Pimpernel Water.

Pimpernel is a most wholesome plant, and often used in European countries for the purpose of whitening the complexion; it is there in so high reputation, that it is said generally, that it ought to be continually on the toilet of every lady who cares for the brightness of her skin.

Eau de Veau.

Boil a calf's foot in four quarts of river water till it is reduced to half the quantity, Add half a pound of rice, and boil it with crum of white bread steeped in milk, a pound of fresh butter and the whites of five fresh eggs; mix with them a small quantity of camphor and alum, and distil the whole. This recipe may be strongly recommended; it is most beneficial to the skin, which it lubricates and softens to a very comfortable degree. The best manner of distilling these ingredients is in the *balneum mariæ;* that is, in a bottle placed in boiling water.

Rose Water.

Put some roses into water, add to them a few drops of acid; the vitriolic acid seems to be preferable to any—soon the water will assume both the colour and perfume of the roses.

Another.

Take two pounds of rose leaves, place them on a napkin tied round the edges of a basin filled with hot water, and put a dish of cold water upon the leaves; keep the bottom water hot, and change the water at top as soon as it begins to grow warm; by this kind of distillation you will extract a great quantity of the essential oil of the roses by a process which cannot be expensive, and will prove very beneficial.

Virgin Milk.

A publication of this kind would certainly be looked upon as an imperfect performance, if we omitted to say a few words upon this famous cosmetic. It consists of a tincture of benjoin, precipitated by water. The tincture of benjoin is obtained by taking a certain quantity of that gum, pouring spirits of wine upon it, and boiling it till it becomes a rich tincture. If you pour a few drops of this tincture into a glass of water, it will produce a mixture which will assume all the appearance of milk, and retain a very agreeable perfume. If the face is washed with this mixture, it will, by calling the purple stream of the blood to the external fibres of the epidermis, produce on the cheeks a beautiful rosy colour; and, if left on the face to dry, it will render it clear and brilliant. It also removes spots, freckles, pimples, erysipelatous eruptions, &c. &c. if they have not been of long standing on the skin.

Lavender Water.

Take four handfuls of dried lavender flowers, and sprinkle on them one quart of brandy, the same quantity of white wine and rose-water;

leave them to remain six days in a large bottle well corked up; let the liquor be distilled and poured off.

Sweet-scented Water.

This agreeably-scented water is not only a pleasant cosmetic, but also of great use in nervous disorders.

Put one quart of rose-water, and the same quantity of orange-water, into a large and wide-mouthed glass; strew upon it two handfuls of jessamine flowers, put the glass in the *balneum mariæ*, or on a slow fire, and when it is distilled, add to it a scruple of musk and the same quantity of ambergris.

Eau d'Ange.

Pound in a mortar fifteen cloves and one pound of cinnamon, and put the whole into a quart of water, with four grains of anniseed; let it stand over a charcoal fire twenty-four hours, then strain off the liquor, and put it up for use. This perfume is most excellent, and will do well for the hands, face, and hair, to which it communicates a very agreeable scent.

Remedy for the Toothach.

In two drachms of rectified spirits of wine dissolve one drachm of camphor, five grains of prepared opium, and ten drops of oil of box; mix them well, and keep it well corked for use. If the pain arise from a hollow tooth, four or five drops on cotton to be put into the tooth; or six or seven drops to be put on cotton into the ear on the side where the pain is felt. Should the patient not feel easier in a quarter of an hour, the same may be repeated. It has never failed on the second application.

An excellent Eye-water.

Take six ounces of rectified spirits of wine, dissolve in it one drachm of camphor, and half a pint of elder-flower water. Wash the eyes night and morning with this liquid; it clears the vision, and strengthens the sight.

Dentifrice.

The following is one of the best recipes for tooth-powder:—

Take of prepared chalk six ounces, cassia powder, half an ounce, orris-root, an ounce. These are to be well mixed, and may be coloured with red lake, or any other innocent substance, according to the fancy of the user. This dentifrice is to be used with a firm brush every morning; the teeth should also be brushed before going to bed, but it is seldom necessary to use the powder more than once a day.

THE END.

www.ingramcontent.com/pod-product-compliance
Lightning Source LLC
LaVergne TN
LVHW011205110826
845150LV00006B/1324

* 9 7 8 1 4 2 5 5 1 8 5 4 7 *